THE
BHAGAVAD GITA
101

A modern, practical guide,
plain and simple

MATTHEW S. BARNES

ALSO BY MATTHEW BARNES

1. **The Zen-nish Series:**
   (amazon.com/author/matthewbarnes)
   The Tao Te Ching 101
   Albert Einstein, Zen Master
   The Tao Te Ching 201
   Jesus Christ, Zen Master
   Dr. Seuss, Zen Master
   Willy Wonka, Zen Master
   Mark Twain, Zen Master
2. **Ancient Egyptian Enlightenment Series:**
   (amazon.com/author/matthewbarnes)
   The Emerald Tablet 101
   The Hermetica 101
   The Kybalion 101
3. **Hindu Enlightenment Series:**
   The Upanishads 101
   The Bhagavad Gita 101
4. **Investing Series (Zen-vesting)**
   (amazon.com/author/matthewbarnes)
   Investing 101
   Investing 201
5. **Novels** (amazon.com/author/msbarnes)
   Folie¿ (a creepy, psychological thriller)
   Meet Frank King (psychological thriller)

DEDICATION

I dedicate this work to those who have the gumption to think for themselves—such a feat is not easy in this world of ours.

I also dedicate this work to all of those who have suffered at the hands of religious intolerance. We all want the freedom to search for our own truths. We all want the freedom to worship and believe in our own ways. Yet there are so many out there who do not wish to grant the same religious freedom to others that they so earnestly and sincerely desire for themselves.

CONTENTS

INTRODUCTION

The Hindu religion is so old and so vast in scope that there is not a single "Bible" (so-to-speak) that encompasses all of the beliefs and practices of the religion. Instead, Hindu beliefs have been spread out over such an expanse of time, and laid down into so many separate scriptures, that if all the individual works were bound into a single volume, that single volume would be hundreds of thousands of pages long. Hinduism is possibly the oldest and most complete religious philosophy in existence, covering an extremely wide variety of spiritual topics and approaches to the spiritual path. The Hindu wise men of old felt the truth of reality to be far too vast for a single book to be able to encapsulate.

That being said, there is one work, the *Bhagavad Gita*, that is considered to be a compact summary of Hindu teachings—a kind of "Cliff's Notes" for the Hindu religion. In only 700 verses, the *Bhagavad Gita* succinctly outlines the culmination of all Hindu beliefs. For this reason, the *Gita*, as it is affectionately referred to, is considered to be the flagship scripture, the cornerstone teaching of the Hindu religion. Written about 200 years before Christ (though it had existed for much longer orally), the *Gita* is actually a small part of a much bigger work called the *Prasthana Trayi*.

The *Bhagavad Gita* (or "Song of Life") is meant to be a comprehensive guidebook to the human condition. We have all, I'm sure, wished at one point or another that life came with a guidebook. For the Hindus, the *Gita* is exactly that—

the blueprint for correct living in a tumultuous and ever-changing world.

We all want to know why we are here. Is there a purpose, a reason we are here? Is there a Higher Power? Is there more to life than what we now see and sense? Is there a reason for all this suffering as a human being? Is there a way to correctly wade our way through? Do we have an existence after the death of our bodies?

There is a television show called *The Good Place* (spoiler alert) where several humans die and go to the "Good Place". Only it turns out that they are not in the Good Place. You eventually find out that though it looks like they are in the Good Place, and they are told they are in the Good Place, they are actually in the Bad Place, being tortured for all of eternity with petty little dramas and moral dilemmas and the like— much like life on earth.

According to the *Gita*, this example is spot on. The reason life is so darn hard is because material existence actually *is* the Bad Place. We are stuck in a prison, basically, and need instructions on how to get out. Our lives are filled with ethical and moral struggles and dilemmas, constant dramas and storms and losses, along with philosophical conundrums, including a crisis of identity. The *Bhagavad Gita* lays out before us and walks us through the issues we face daily as human beings, then addresses a path to properly navigating those obstacles. The *Gita* wrestles with questions about our identity, how we should live, the purpose of life, and so on. The teachings encompass the entire spiritual and ethical struggle of humankind.

According to the *Gita,* we are here to live a life worth living in a world in which that is very hard to do. If you fail, you repeat with another life. If you succeed, you join the source of creation—you go to the "Good Place", freeing yourself from more rounds in the "Bad Place".

The first thing you may notice with the last paragraph is the Hindu belief in reincarnation. The second thing you may notice is that the idea of Hell in this religion is not the burning Hell of many modern religions, but is actually the material world. We are already in Hell, so to speak, and the worst thing that can happen to us is that we have to return to earth in another physical form to try again.

Interestingly, the *Gita* does not offer a single path to salvation. Instead, it outlines a couple of main paths and also mentions a multitude of others. Which path is correct? They all are. All paths lead to the same place, and your best path depends on your individual personality. You need to choose and follow the path that best fits your individual propensities and inclinations. In fact, according to Krishna, you can even be an atheist or an agnostic and still find liberation if you serve others selflessly or come to understand the universe through knowledge (see my other work, *Albert Einstein, Zen Master* for an example of a knowledge-based approach). Note how different this is from modern religions that teach a single path as the one and only way.

The two main paths are (1) seeing God (or whatever you want to call It) as a personified figure, or (2) (in Star Wars terminology) as a Force or Intelligence that creates and binds all that exists. Again, either way is fine, it just depends on your temperament. Find the path that best suits you. Each person is born with different personalities and tendencies—the Path is therefore not a one-size-fits-all solution.

At one point in the *Gita*, Krishna explicitly states that *all* spiritual paths, if they are approached earnestly, eventually lead to Him. This, of course, is, once again, very different from the teachings of most modern religions. Western religions tend to personify God and choose devotion as their main path. Eastern religions tend to see what we call God as Consciousness or the Intelligence of the Universe, a Power that cannot be personified.

Further, the Hindu religion believes that over the course of human history, many Messiahs have come to us (the Hindus call them Avatars). Krishna is the Avatar (the Jesus) of the *Bhagavad Gita*; God in human form. Because the Hindus believe that many Avatars have come to help us over the lifetime of the human race, they have no problem in accepting Jesus and Buddha and others as Avatars just as important as their Krishna. This again can be seen in stark contrast to the modern and especially Western religions where each religion's Messiah has to be the one, the only, and the true Messiah. This may be one reason Gandhi, a Hindu, once said he very much liked Christ, but not so much Christians, for he often found Christians to be very unlike their Christ.

The *Gita* is a call to action for us to meet head-on all the struggles and obligations of material existence, but at the same time find the grander purpose of existence. A hero is defined by the *Gita* not in terms of physical abilities, but in terms of our commitment to following our Dharma (purpose) here on the earth, on the battlefield of life.

Speaking of battlefields, the *Gita* uses war as an analogy to our struggles in the material world. The story is of a hero, Arjuna, who must fight in a war he does not want to participate in. Krishna tells Arjuna that he *must* fight. He has to. He can't just give up and play dead. It's just not an option. If he does this, he'll simply die (eventually) and have to take on another body and try again. No, he has to fight. It's what he's here to do. He has to take on the struggles, duties and moral dilemmas of this world, and through that struggle find the path that leads to the transcendence of this world. It is Arjuna's purpose on earth. It is why he is here.

The battle is not external, though. It is not black versus white, liberal versus conservative, America versus the Middle East, one religion versus another ... no, the battle is within. It is the battle between what is good and right versus what is not, just like the spiritual Jihad of the Islamic religion. At stake is the spiritual struggle against our own lower nature, the ego.

The personal moral confusion and angst at the heart of being human has to be addressed and studied. Arjuna must fight against and transcend his ego and the social norms of the world around him in order to find That which is true and permanent and real—what Krishna calls Absolute Reality. This is why we are here. It is what we are meant to do. And until we do it, we are stuck here. This is why we must fight. We are on a battlefield of moral struggle, fighting the war within. And we fight over and over until we succeed.

I have used the movie *Groundhog Day* as an analogy in past works, and it fits again here. In the movie, Bill Murray's character lives a single day over and over and over until he lives not for the self, not from the perspective of the ego, but out of service to others. Follow the *Gita* as a guide, live as it tells you to, and you break free of the cycle of material existence.

One of the main issues humans face is that we suffer on an almost ongoing basis and want an end to that suffering, but seek it in the things of this world. We seek an end to our suffering through the pursuit of money and power and acclaim. If we get enough of these things, we may even give up the spiritual struggle because we have found at least a little comfort in the material world. In *Gita* terms, we actually become a bit comfortable, a bit complacent living in this prison, and we accept it and cease our searching. The *Gita* warns us against this, as this world and all its niceties are transient. Money doesn't last, and neither does power or fame. Life doesn't last, and in fact, neither does death. There is only one thing that is permanent, and if you suffer long enough you will eventually seek it out—this marks the true beginning of your spiritual sojourn.

As mentioned before, there are two main paths outlined in the *Gita* - seeing God as a personified entity (as in the Jewish, Christian and Muslim religions) and seeing God in a non-personified way (as in Taoism, Zen and Buddhism). The lessons of the *Gita* can be studied in either context. In the personified version, Krishna is God incarnate, instructing Arjuna personally. In the non-personified view, Krishna is our inner voice, our Soul, our inner Guide, trying to guide us to liberation, what the Hindus refer to as Moksha. Moksha is already ours, say the Hindus, the Buddhists, and Zen masters, we just aren't able to see it because we have a form of spiritual amnesia. This amnesia is at the heart of the *Gita*. Regain your memory and deliverance is assured. Krishna is trying to restore Arjuna's memory in this work. It is almost the entire purpose of the work. Arjuna (humankind) has forgotten who and what he is and where he has come from. Krishna is attempting to help him remember. Interestingly, Moksha is not something to be attained - it can't be attained, only realized. It's already ours. Realize it and the war is over.

In my Zen works, I went over a scenario that occurred in a Zen school. A student appeared before his master, completely stricken. He begged his master to just give him the answers, to deliver him from this world because he had reached a level of misery that he could no longer handle. The Zen master instructs the student that he doesn't have the power to deliver him, that each student must walk the path alone. Additionally, he told the student that "Even now, even in your present situation, the answer is before you. Liberation is as close as your own breath." This also coincides with the lessons of the *Gita*—every situation, every struggle, every emotion, and every thought we have presents before us as a lesson to learn that can lead us either further into attachment to the material world or, conversely, into transcending it, depending on how we choose to react. We can either attach to the emotions and outcomes of life or be transformed by them.

The Gita rejects the monastic life, for we are here to participate in the world and to help each other advance. Avoid life and we avoid the very lessons and struggles that are meant to propel us to higher and higher levels of consciousness. In struggling with life, in trying to obtain money and power and acceptance, we eventually come to see it all as ephemeral, as transitory, and begin searching for a way out—a better way, a permanent state of tranquility. Become a monk, renounce your life and such battles and struggles may not reach you.

Further, the *Gita* is against rituals performed mechanically. Such rituals do not propel us to higher ideals—they are merely outward pretenses that lead nowhere. Singing hymns or reciting scripture as loud as possible on Sundays isn't enough, you have to *live* the message. The *Gita* is all about action. And again, it openly accepts multiple ways of life, best fitted to each individual seeker. The *Gita* admonishes us to resist the "my way only" view, which is just the desire of the ego that we are trying to transcend, and asks us to consider all ways honestly traveled as valid paths.

At the very center of the *Gita* is the idea of doing your duty as best you can but not focusing on the outcome. "You are a vehicle of something higher" it is saying, "concentrate on doing your duty, concentrate on doing what is right, and leave the results to the Universe." This idea is portrayed very well in the movie *The Legend of Bagger Vance* which is actually based around the *Gita*. At the end of the movie (spoiler alert), the main character refuses to do something he considers wrong, even though those around him, even his opponents, tell him is okay. If he follows their advice, he could actually win the golf tournament he is playing against the two greatest golfers of his age. If he doesn't, at best he would only tie. He chooses to do what is right, and after he hits his last shot says, "Well, I couldn't have hit it any better than that". He did what was right. He did it to the best of his ability. The results were out of his hands, and none of his concern.

And that is the way we are all to live our lives. We are to do our duty, do what is right, give it all of our attention, do it the best we can (like a Zen master participating in a tea ceremony), and have no care for the result. Money, power, acclaim—we don't do what we do for those rewards. Doing what is right, the best we can, ultimately *is* the reward. Doing a good deed because we think we will be noticed, or receive a reward, or become rich is still earthly, prison-level thinking.

Also at the heart of the *Gita* is the idea that God is in each of us. God is in all that exists, and all that exists is in God. The fruits of our labors are His, not our own, so we are to concentrate on the action and surrender the results to Him (or if you prefer, to It).

Our world, says the *Gita*, is one of infinite variety and change. Life does not last. Neither does death. We see the world as we are, not as it is. We give meaning and shape to what has none and we create boundaries where they do not exist—all are tricks of the ego we have become so attached to. *We* create friends and enemies. *We* create right and wrong. *We* create our own truths and let them define us.

In summary, according to the *Gita*, life is rough. It is meant to be. It does have its moments, but overall it is simply a rollercoaster ride of drama and emotion. Every good event or time in your life will be followed with bad. Just look at the erratic chart of the stock market if you need proof of this. Every upturn is followed by a drawdown, and every drawdown is followed by a recovery. Even when you do find happiness, it won't last. It just won't. Life is supposed to be this way—it is the whole point. It is pushing us painfully along until we begin to question the value of material gains. Life is moving us to desire something more, to desire something better—

to seek something more substantial and permanent than the treasures of this world.

So how do we get out of this prison? We all eventually do. It is simply the maturing process of the human soul. We all get there, just at our own pace. But the *Gita* can speed that process up for us by mapping out the terrain of our prison and showing us the means to escape. So that no one is left out, multiple plans are laid out before us. Take the path that best suits you and the song that vibrates and flows through all that exists comes into view—as a personified Entity if you prefer, or as a non-personified Intelligence if that best fits your nature. Suffering then ceases in all of its guises, even here and now in this life, and with the death of our bodies, we merge with that Song.

How do you know that one has obtained such a state? Such a person will be friendly and kind to all. Honor and shame will be the same to them, as will wealth or poverty. Such a person will be beyond heat and cold, pleasure or pain—they may still experience such things, but will give them no mind. Such a person will have found the permanent behind this world of impermanence. They now see the entire Universe pervaded by a single Universal Consciousness or Intelligence, and they now live in a world of marvel that they have fallen in love with.

As with my other works, I am going for the forest, not the trees. I do not interpret this work academically. I do not portray the lessons in the form of a physical battle between two armies as the original *Gita* does. Each person in the *Gita* represents a different aspect of earthly struggle, or a mental process for escaping—I don't go into all of that. Again, I am going for the big picture, the overall themes and lessons. If you want a more academic interpretation, I suggest you explore the resources at the end of this work.

Further, because the Hindu concepts are so vast, being laid down over such an extended period of time, I do not even attempt to approach each and every aspect of its teachings. Such a feat would encompass thousands and thousands of pages and would defeat my purpose of a simple, direct and compact delivery.

I also do not use a lot of Hindu names and explanations. I have to in certain areas, but overall I have tried to place the lessons of the *Gita* into modern language and modern terms in hopes that they will be better understood by the current population of this world. And, as always, this is my current understanding, my own interpretation.

"There are hundreds of paths up the mountain, all leading to the same place, so it doesn't matter which path you take. The only person wasting time is the one who runs around the mountain, telling everyone that his or her path is wrong."
-Hindu Proverb

CHAPTER 1

The Dark Night of the Soul

Arjuna paused.

He looked before him and all around him— life had become nothing but a battle; an ongoing war filled with frustration, sadness, and despair. There were moments of happiness, to be sure, but it never lasted. Gone was the bright-eyed enthusiasm and certainty of youth; in their place had risen doubt and discontent.

There were bills to pay, mouths to feed, and no end to the drama and emotional storms swirling all around and within him. Both his work and family life were endlessly stressful and there seemed to him no end, no escape from the storms. No matter how hard he had fought, no matter how much he had been able to achieve, there still seemed to be nothing but further struggles ahead. He'd overcome so many obstacles only to find a new one had taken its place each time. Would he ever be able to rest in success? Would he ever find peace? Would he ever be content? It seemed impossible. Life seemed pointless.

What little success he had achieved was always short-lived, fleeting, and it never made him happy, not truly. At least not for long. No matter how much he achieved, there was always a desire for more. Even if everything seemed to be going his way, his mind was still able to find new issues to fret over. There was simply no end, no way out of his depression. Life was just not worth the struggle.

Arjuna was also getting older and was now having to deal with illness. Not the short-lived illnesses of a young man, but the chronic, permanent illnesses of a body that was wearing out, working its way towards death, which frightened Arjuna to no end. Death was always at the back of his mind. In youth, he felt he would live forever; now he was acutely aware of the looming certainty of his death.

Finally, he'd watched lovers come and go, and he'd seen loved ones succumb to illnesses and death, tragedies that affected him more than he had the capacity to handle.

What good is all this? he thought. *What point is there in going on? What good is a struggle that never ends? A struggle that leads to naught in the end? A struggle that can never be won? You struggle and then you die. Where's the point in that? Even when I was wealthy I still wasn't happy. Now food has lost its flavor, diamonds have lost their glitter—all that once seemed so enticing has become colorless ... flat ... dull.*

Despair overwhelmed Arjuna and he grew weak. *There really is no point*, he thought. *No reason to go on. None whatsoever.*

"The dark night of the soul is when you have lost the flavor of life but have not yet gained the fullness of divinity. So it is that we must weather that dark time, the period of transformation when what is familiar has been taken away and the new richness is not yet ours."
-Ram Dass

CHAPTER 2

The Immortal Soul

Krishna, Arjuna's friend and confidant, sensed Arjuna's desperation and asked, "What is wrong? What in the world has made you so upset?"

"What good is it? Any of it?" Arjuna answered. "Life is nothing but an endless struggle, and one that can't be won. What is the point of continuing? If there is one, I cannot see it. All that I have desired or loved has passed away in the end, or will. All happiness is fleeting. It is just not worth the effort. Life is … pointless."

Krishna smiled. "I have been waiting a long time, Arjuna, to hear such words. I believe you are finally ready …"

Arjuna looked up at Krishna quizzically. "You are a good friend, Krishna, but I see no point in you trying to persuade me to go on. No matter how hard I struggle, I seem to get nowhere. You have been my friend for years, you know all I have been through. I have given it all I have within me and have no more to give. I am exhausted. I am miserable, and I feel that I have made almost no headway at all. The battle is without end. The only logical decision is to quit. Life has no point—in the end, it is empty. It can't be won. It seems as unfulfilling to me as a corpse." He hung his head in defeat.

"You have finally made it, my friend," Krishna said, beaming gently. "You have finally reached the point where I may be able to step in and help."

Arjuna was puzzled. "What are you getting at?" he asked.

"We have been friends, as you have said, for many years," said Krishna, "and I now have to confess that I am more than what you have come to know Me as. Until now, there was no way I could help, so I kept my true identity to Myself. You were too caught up in the niceties of this existence for me to guide you beyond them. Wealth, power, fame—they were the rewards you were attached to, the rewards you had set your heart upon. What I am about to tell you would have seemed, at the time, bland and tasteless next to the splendors of this world that you were so fond of. But now that you have found the transient nature of this world, the ephemeral qualities of the treasures within it, you may actually be ready. You may actually now be able to hear what I have come to tell you."

A glimmer of hope emerged within Arjuna's eyes. "I truly hope you have something for me, for I feel I cannot continue in this current state. Life has lost all meaning for me."

"That is because," Krishna went on, "you have given this world your own meaning instead of following its lead. You have lived egocentrically, wishing life to provide you, as an individual, with all you have wished for. Life simply does not work that way. Life operates for the good of the whole, not for the good of the individual. There *is* meaning to life, there *is* purpose, but life's purpose goes beyond your individual concerns alone. The material world contains no lasting treasures, as you have come to find, yet you clung to it and gave yourself hope that you would find happiness and contentment and meaning within it. The greed of your ego blinded you to the abundance of wealth beyond this existence. The material world *is* a corpse, Arjuna, and within it there are no lasting benefits. *What propels the material corpse though,*

That is a treasure unto Itself. This world would be nothing but an empty, inanimate shell were it not for the Intelligence, the Force that permeates every aspect of its being. The corpse you have found before you is driven by an Intelligence that is invisible to the human eye yet still observable in Its actions. You have focused only on the shell and found it empty and meaningless. Focus now on the animating Force that guides it and life will begin for you anew—you will be reborn within a new reality."

"But how?" Arjuna asked.

"Come to see the material forms before you as secondary and the Intelligence that animates those forms as primary. Make the Intelligence that runs the universe your focus and the miracle of life will unfold at your feet. Do this and you will never look upon this world in the same manner again. The Intelligence of life is a marvel to behold, and unlike material treasures, its bounty does not come and go—it can never be used up, lost, taken, or depleted. The more of Its wonder you are able to realize, the more It will reveal to you. Instead of shrinking with use, It enlarges. Find It and there is no end to Its bounty. Share It and It will shower you with more than you could ever need or hope for. Seek It and the contentment and peace and comfort you so earnestly desire will be yours for all of eternity. You fell in love with the material world, Arjuna, and have finally found it to be a corpse. Now focus your attention on the Intelligence that animates the corpse and all suffering will vanish like the darkness of night when the light of day emerges from its slumber."

Arjuna straightened up, enthralled. "Please, do go on! Please!"

"What animates this living world, Arjuna? What allows your corpse to move its arms, blink its eyes and digest its food? What moves life through the unending cycles of winter, spring, summer, and fall? What moves the day through morning, noon, afternoon, and night? What moves a living being through youth, adulthood, old age and eventually death? What makes the stars shine and the planets to spin and circle the sun with unerring precision? What Force is it that holds atoms and matter together in coherent patterns?"

"I see what you mean," Arjuna admitted. "But isn't this Intelligence you speak of just the laws of nature? Isn't it just the laws of gravity and the like? Isn't it just chemical bonds and chemical reactions and the forces of attraction that do these things, simply by their own inherent natures?"

"That *is* the Intelligence of which I speak, Arjuna, but you have taken It for granted. You have set your focus on the manifest but paid no attention to the mover of the manifest. You have devoted yourself to the seen, yet remained ignorant of the Unseen that makes the seen possible. You are like a child at a puppet show, oblivious to the animator of the puppets you see moving before you. You can afford to do so no longer. Tell me, Arjuna, what is this "nature" you speak of? What do you know of it? What is the essence of That which creates and moves entire universes? What is the Force, the Intelligence that animates and holds together dimensions unending? What can you tell me about the origin of chemical bonds and the laws of gravity?"

"I only know … that it all exists," Arjuna admitted. "I know that things move. I know that life exists. I know the stars remain in their correct place. I know the sun marches daily across the sky. I know that I can walk and talk and laugh and cry. But I guess I do not know exactly how all of that occurs. I do not know what propels it all into being. Or why ..."

"Exactly," said Krishna. "The manifest phenomena of this world are knowable, but receive their being from That which is not. This nature you speak of cannot be defined, only observed in action, for It exists beyond human perception; even beyond human conception. Formless, It pervades all forms. Eternal, it was never born and can never die. We see It in action all day long, but never pay attention to the mystery of Its being. It is constantly before our very nose, yet remains the farthest thing from our minds. That, Arjuna, is the mental mistake you must correct if you are to free yourself from the struggles of this world. The living Intelligence of this world, what you refer to as nature, is a Song that you can hear but never see, at least not with human eyes; a mystery you can perceive as existing, but never fully comprehend. And *It* needs to be the focus of your attention, not the material forms you see before you. You can no longer afford for Its existence to remain in the shadow of Its creations. This is the alteration in focus that must occur within your mind in order for you to advance beyond the knowledge of this material existence of form alone. You have come to know the material world and found an empty corpse. Come now to know the unseen Intelligence that drives the form and you will find Life Itself."

Arjuna began to weep. "Please ... please continue. I feel hope growing within me and it is impelling me to go on."

"And go on you must!" Krishna exclaimed. "The only way out of this war is through, My friend. The only escape from the Hell you are trapped in is to rise above it, and to do so you must first wade through all the dramas and moral dilemmas of your life. Your struggles are specific to you and you *must* engage them—you *must* continue the struggle. Your frustrations themselves will eventually lead you to a reality that exists beyond them. You have already made a giant leap with the help of those struggles, have you not? Through those struggles have you not found the emptiness of physical existence? The only way to lose, Arjuna, is to quit, so you *must* go on. Life is a battle—it is meant to be. It is not fair—it is meant not to be. It is a war that you are here to fight—it is why you are here. Fight, persist, and you *will* eventually triumph, and then you will understand the why of it all. For now you will have to trust what I am telling you. Keep going, Arjuna, for you are close. Your mind is on the verge of a great conversion. You have reached the Dark Night of the Soul, and I have come to guide you to the dawn beyond. You have found the emptiness of your current existence and you mourn for its loss. It is all you have known—I understand. Let me guide you now to what comes next, and I give you my word that you will never mourn again."

"But … more struggle?" Arjuna asked, despondent. "What if I cannot? What if I simply cannot? What if I am unable to continue? What if I am done in? I feel so weak. So desolate. What will become of me if I cannot go on?"

"Then with the death of this body, you will be reborn into another human form—you will get to try again. And where is the fear in that? You have done it before, Arjuna—many, many times before. You can do it again. You are immortal, Arjuna. You cannot be harmed. Fail and you try again. Succeed, and when your current form passes, you come to Me."

"I am immortal?" Arjuna asked. "I come to You? How do you mean? I am not sure I understand."

"Is this Nature you speak of only to be found in the universe around you? Are only the stars and planets imbued with and animated by this living Intelligence? Or is this same intelligence to be found within you as well? Do you not live and breathe and move? Are there not chemical reactions occurring within you? Do you not also contain the same living Force that moves the universe?"

"Go on," Arjuna begged.

"What you call Nature is the immortal Soul of the world, the Immortal Essence within all things. Consciousness exists within that Essence—Consciousness *is* that Essence— and you *are* that Consciousness, not this mortal form your consciousness inhabits, not the mortal corpse that you have come to believe to be the self. With the death of the body, your Consciousness goes on, dropping the body just as easily as one sheds clothes. Complete your journey, and at the time of your bodily death, your earthly struggles will end—your Consciousness will come to Me. Complete it not and you try again. Either way, what is there to fear? You are immortal, Arjuna, you go on. Not your body but your Consciousness, your Essence, your Soul. No sword can cut It, no fire can burn It. It was never born and It can never die. You can neither kill the consciousness of another nor can your consciousness be killed. You are not your body and you are not your ego. You are a Consciousness that existed long before It inhabited a human form, and that Consciousness will go on long after this current form has died and turned to dust. Weep not for the living nor for the dead, for in Consciousness, there is no death, only life. There are no dangers to be found on this path. Nothing can harm you, there is nothing to fear. You cannot see this yet because you are still trapped in human form, with a body and an ego that you have identified with. But this is just not so. You have achieved the first step—you have come to see the emptiness of material existence and it is time for you to move beyond it. You are not who and what you thought you were, Arjuna, and the time has come for you to see that. You have grown weary of the ego, of the lower self. Now it is time for you to experience the higher Self."

"But ... if I don't achieve liberation now, I have to start over?"

"Not from the beginning, Arjuna," Krishna answered. "No effort, no accomplishment is ever lost, My friend. If you do not reach liberation in this lifetime, you do not start over from the beginning in your next incarnation. You begin your next incarnation from the level you were able to reach during this lifetime."

"Still ..." Arjuna said, "to have to go through all this again ... no ... I do not want that. Please, friend, please tell me how to go forward. What am I to do? I want to obtain liberation in this incarnation!"

"Continue!" said Krishna. "That is the answer, the only answer. Keep going. You must go on. You must continue the struggle. All that comes before you is life leading you to the ultimate truth. Life has finally led you to see the pointlessness of material gain. Now you must continue, for Life Itself will show you the next step—the struggle *is* the path. So continue the struggle, live, and with every obstacle that presents itself before you, look for the lesson behind it, the realization life is trying to lead you toward."

"But how?" asked Arjuna. "How do my frustrations, all the obstacles in my path lead me forward?"

"You used to desire gold, did you not?" Krishna asked.

"I did," Arjuna affirmed.

"And why do you not now?" asked Krishna.

"Because there was no point in it," answered Arjuna. "I would accrue some, then I would lose almost all I had accrued. Even when I had enough, it still didn't make me happy."

"Exactly," said Krishna. "This was life leading you to understand the futility of earthly wealth. In a similar manner life will challenge you to reassess *all* that you currently hold dear."

"Oh," said Arjuna. "I see."

"Remember this at all times:" Krishna added, "The way out of this world is through it. You must trudge on!"

Arjuna nodded his comprehension, unable to speak.

"So live!" said Krishna, "And as you do so, focus your attention on the present moment, on the task at hand. The Soul of the world lives only in the here and now, only in the moment before you. Only here can It be observed. Only here can It be accessed. Only here can it be felt, entered. The past and the future are mere projections of the ego mind, but the present is real—it is the gateway to perceiving the living Intelligence that contains the answers you seek. Remain rooted in the present moment, lose yourself in the task at hand, and the constant babbling of the ego mind will begin to fade and the silent void of Eternity will finally be able to edge Its way in."

"But ... but," Arjuna began. "Exactly what is it that I am to do? What actions am I to take part in? What kind of job do you want me to pursue? Do I need to pray? Do You want sacrifices? Do You want me to perform rituals?"

"The only prayer I need is your action. The only sacrifice I ask for is the sacrifice of your life, well-lived, in service to others. The only ritual I desire is for you to perform the tasks that come naturally for you in this life, and for you to do them well. Use your talents to help the world around you. Do what is right, without hesitation, and you will find the way. Your intent comes to Me, Arjuna, nothing else. Results are out of your hands, they are only in Mine. But the effort, the intent, that is sweet as honey to Me. I use your talents for My purpose, so do them well and leave the rest to Me. Give a homeless man a dollar and if he spends it on alcohol, that is not your concern. Do you understand? If you give with the honest intent of helping, you have done your part. What he does with your generosity, that is on him."

"I do," said Arjuna. "I understand."

"This goes for all that you do, Arjuna. A job half-done is half-pleasing to me. Pray all you want, quote as many scriptures as you please, do all the honorable things you like, but if done for any other reason than a pure deed done well it won't come to Me. So keep your mind off thoughts of personal gain or reward. Deeds done for attention or earthly rewards produce only earthly results, but deeds done for Me produce unending returns. There are two entities existing within you, Arjuna, your ego (which does not even exist—it is a trick of the mind, as you will soon come to see) and your Soul (which is eternal). The one you feed the most is the one that wins.

Feed the ego and you will remain trapped within its prison walls, both in this lifetime and all others that may be to come. Shake off the ego, starve it out and a higher level of Mind emerges. With the death of the body, such a Consciousness comes to Me. This is the way."

"Such a person that follows this path," asked Arjuna. "what are they like?"

"They give for the sake of giving, without thought of acclaim or reward. They do their duty in this life, impervious to praise or blame, honor or shame. Seeing the Immortal beyond the form, they see no difference between one object and another. In all they do, they address the Spirit not the form, the Intelligence not the corpse. In Spirit, they have found that all are One, All are Me—there are no individual lives; not in the way you have come to believe. Even the concepts of self and other have dissolved into non-reality for a person who has found Me. Such a person endures heat and cold patiently, knowing the unpleasantries of this world to be temporary. In either poverty or riches they are content. Free from desire, and greed, and anger they rest in the permanent never-ending Source of this impermanent existence. They now have All—there is nothing more for them to obtain—yet still their journey continues, for there is no end to the depths of what I am. Finding Me, they have reached a world of marvel, and they have fallen in love with that marvel—they treasure It beyond all else. Such a person is dear to Me, Arjuna—such a person is as immeasurable and immortal as I."

Arjuna hugged his friend. "Truly, my spirits are lifted. I am ready."

"Rejoice, Arjuna!" Krishna said, "For your liberation is near. But never forget that the way out is through. In the midst of all the dramas and dilemmas and moral conundrums of life, that is where you find Me. Arise! Fight! Come to me! Fight and you will come to understand more than any holy work ever written. Arise like a fire that burns all before it and fulfill your purpose, fulfill your destiny! Shed your self-pity and adopt the mindset of a warrior! This world is yours to conquer and you are almost there. The end is near. You can do it! And I will be there to help, every step of the way!"

"You will be there? You will help?"

"I will never leave you, Arjuna, never. Though up to now you were unaware, you have never taken a single step on your path alone, and you never will."

"Blessed is the person who has struggled. He has found life."
-The Gospel of Thomas

CHAPTER 3

Dharma

"What is it, Arjuna?" Krishna asked. "Your elation seems to have been short-lived?"

"I must admit that I was initially excited ... beyond excited, to be honest. You succinctly pointed out the very struggles and dilemmas that are at the heart of being human, or at least the struggles and dilemmas that had overtaken me personally, draining me of my will to go on. And you also outlined the solution, which made sense to me at the time, but ..."

"Go on," said Krishna. "It is normal to have questions. You are not upsetting Me."

"Well, it is just that you seem to be saying that knowledge is the antidote for my angst, the key to escaping my anxiety and depression. That knowing my true nature to be eternal, not mortal, means the end of my suffering and the beginning of my liberation."

"That is correct," said Krishna. "So what is the problem?"

"If knowledge is the answer, and I now have that knowledge, do I really need to go on? Do I really need to continue the struggle? Do I still have to work? It seems contradictory to say that knowledge is the answer, but then say that even though I have it I still need to go on with my duties to reach salvation."

"I see where your understanding has gotten caught," answered Krishna. "First of all, knowledge, ultimately, *is* the answer, but you have only begun to understand. You have not yet experienced the truth for yourself, as you eventually must. It is still but a concept for you, merely something that I have told you. When you do experience it for yourself, you will come to realize that action is the centerpiece, the linchpin of the material universe of which you are still a part. Movement in this material existence means life, stillness equates to death. If your heart stops beating, you die. If water stops flowing, it stagnates. If atoms stop spinning, matter will cease to exist. If the universe stops evolving, it will fall apart."

"I see," said Arjuna.

"Knowledge delivers you from the belief that you are mortal," Krishna continued, "but action is still needed as long as you have a body, as long as you exist in this earthly realm. And your actions bring you into contact with the very questions and dilemmas that you need to face in order to advance you forward. No, even though I have revealed the truth to you, action is still a necessity as long as you exist within the material world. "

"Oh," said Arjuna. "I thought that with knowledge, I might no longer be bound to action."

"Not until you reach the Ultimate," Krishna replied. "Not until you rise above the mortal nature of this world and rejoin the Eternal. Until then, you have a duty to perform that benefits both yourself as well as My own purposes. So no, Arjuna, you are not yet done. You must trudge on. But doing so in the knowledge that you are an eternal being that can no more be harmed than can I should ease your mind in the struggles to come. Such knowledge should impel you to fight without fear, for no harm can come to you, of this I promise."

"It does help! Oh, it does! I just thought …"

"I know what you thought, but it is not the way. I am the maker of all the worlds, Arjuna, and dimensions unending. In all there is, there is nothing I need to do, nothing I need to attain or obtain for I am all, yet I still go on—I still contribute. If I stopped, the world would end. How much lower is your duty? How much less do you have to accomplish? Yet you wish to quit? You make use of my efforts yet balk at contributing your own? Only a thief takes without contributing, and you are not a thief, are you?"

"I am most definitely not!"

"Exactly. So you must go on and contribute your verse to the Song of Life. It is part of your duty. The lower life forms perform their parts instinctively, without intent, but the higher life forms are conscious of their talents, with which they are to contribute. Without knowledge, you live in fear. Your contributions are selfish, geared only for the betterment of your individual situation. Without action, you partake of my contributions but offer none in return. Neither is the path to Me. Do you understand?"

"I think so," Arjuna answered.

"Good. Then I will go on … All forms of life have a purpose in this world—a duty, a 'dharma' to fulfill. The lower life forms, as I have said, perform their duties instinctively. They perform the duties I need of them without thought. The higher life forms, and here I am referring to humans, are in the final stages of the evolution of consciousness, and they must perform their duties voluntarily. They must *choose* to participate, they must *choose* to fulfill their destiny. As a human, you are aware of your own particular talents, and you must eventually *choose* to use them for the benefit of all, to add your own unique verse to the Melody of Life."

"I understand," said Arjuna. "Part of the reason we exist is to contribute."

"Correct," said Krishna. "Humans begin their incarnations lazy, living off the efforts of others. Though fully capable of earning their own livelihood, many choose to remain inert, being fed and clothed by others."

"I have noticed this!" said Arjuna. "There seem to be so many that live off the efforts of others! I often ponder how they are able to survive."

"Over many incarnations," Krishna went on, "these same humans eventually grow to recognize their individual talents and develop and use them, but initially they do so only for their own selfish benefits. Eventually, they will begin to mature beyond the viewpoint of their own individual wants, and needs, and desires and begin using their talents for the betterment of all. Such people have been referred to as "old souls", and rightfully so, for to reach such a level requires many incarnations."

"I have noticed this as well," said Arjuna. "Just as there are those who think only about themselves, there are also some that seem to be nearly selfless."

"Those that refuse to work," said Krishna. "those that refuse to use their talents are not yet on the path to liberation. Those that use their gifts for selfish gains are beginning on the path, for at least they are acting, but they are not quite there either. Only those who have found and developed and used their talents to the best of their ability, and for the good of all, have found the Path that leads to Eternity. Refuse to do

THE BHAGAVAD GITA 101

your duty, or do it, but only for selfish ends, and you are not working for Me. You are serving your own, individual ego. Still attached to that ego, at death you return to serve it once again. You cannot serve two masters, Arjuna, and the master you choose is the master you will get. Choose Me, act without thought of reward, and you break the karmic bonds that bind you to this world. As a human, you have a choice as to your path. You can choose the lower path that will never lead to satisfaction, as you have discovered, or you can choose the higher path that leads to Me."

"So, knowledge is only part of the path. Action is also needed. I understand."

"Correct. But only selfless actions performed without attachment to the results. Even good actions that are performed in hopes of praise or worldly gain are not pure. You must do your duty for the sake of contributing and nothing more if you are ever to find satisfaction. I use your talents to My own benefit, not yours—find your fulfilment in that. Your happiness must be sought from within, never from without. If you seek validation from the external world you will seldom receive it, or keep it. Do not let the external world be your focus, Arjuna. Do not let it shake the peace that exists within you. This is the puzzle you must solve. You must learn how to live within the world and contribute to it while remaining free of its attachments. Until now, you have sought contentment outside of yourself and found only depression and despair. Now look within, the only place you have yet to look. You are a child of two worlds, but only one leads to fulfillment. To find Me, become like Me, for like attracts like. Adopt the mindset of the world and your consciousness merges into its consciousness. Adopt My mindset, and your consciousness will merge with My own, with Your own—you will realize the Root, you will find the Self."

"Become like You?" Arjuna asked. "How in the world am I to do that?"

"I have been instructing you how to accomplish this all along," Krishna answered. "I do not perform my duties for Myself alone. I sacrifice my Self to the greater good and you are to do the same. I give to all without thought of recompense. I perform my duties for sinners and saints alike, flowers and weeds, the awakened and the as-of-yet ignorant. We are all in this together, Arjuna. You and I and all of creation. Join hands and we merge into One. Remain separate and you leave my Grace."

"Leave your Grace?" Arjuna asked. "But You said that You would never leave me. That I never walk alone."

"I do not leave you, Arjuna, but when you choose ego, *you* leave Me. I am still there, but you won't let Me in. As soon as you accept Me, I am there. To accept Me, follow My lead. This, Arjuna, is the virtue of work. This is losing your self in service, and in doing so, finding your higher Self. This is the yoga of action, the way of action. Do you understand?"

"I think so," Arjuna responded.

"It is simple," said Krishna. "Use your talents for the benefit of all and you move beyond the individual and into the Whole."

"Okay. I do think your words are sinking in," Arjuna said. He sat quietly, deep in contemplation. "Do you wish me to teach Your truths to others? Am I to spread your message? Surely there are others in need of hearing Your message."

"In time they will hear the message, but of their own accord, as it was with you. Your job is to become a beacon of hope to others; to lead by example, not by words. Do not attempt to force understanding onto those that are not yet ready, for you will only disturb them—their minds are not yet prepared for the end of their ego, which they still take to be who and what they are. All mature at their own pace—Life Itself will ripen them in good time. Leading by example is the best you can do right now, and is My desire. Those that are ready will take notice, the rest are not your concern—they are Mine. But let not the misunderstanding of the masses shake your own peace. You cannot let the ignorance of those around you dislodge you from the Source, or else you will fall back into worldliness with them. Let the unripe continue their selfish works. Let them continue to encite scriptures that they use to validate their own beliefs and desires. They will eventually overcome their egos. They will come to Me in the end. All do. But their salvation is My job, and theirs, not yours."

Arjuna nodded. "I find that idea hard to follow, but I do understand."

"In trying to save another," Krishna added, "it is hard for your intent to remain pure. Most who try are doing so with egotistical intent. Do you not know religious people who believe that their way and only their way is correct? People that try to force their beliefs onto you?"

"Yes," said Arjuna. "I do know such people."

"This is only ego, Arjuna, and must be avoided. It is nothing but another temptation, another trick of the ego. Further, until you have escaped, what right do you have to instruct another? You have not escaped yourself, yet you feel the ability to lead others? Though your intent is pure, it is all still the folly of the ego, Arjuna."

Arjuna nodded once again.

"So do your duty," Krishna continued, "for Me and for all of creation, and keep your mind off of reward. Leave the results to Me and *I* will be your reward. Find your place in this world and fill it. Do the duty I have given you and leave others to find and fulfill their own. Even if your duty is humble, in its performance you will find salvation, as opposed to doing the duty of another, even if it be grandiose. To fulfill your own duty leads to eternal life. To perform another's duty leads only to rebirth. Be yourself, Arjuna, everyone else is already taken. Are you still with me? For there is one more thing I need to add—one more pitfall I need you to be aware of."

"I think so."

"You must detach yourself from both desire and aversion, for both have their roots in the ego. To desire one thing in life over another is nothing but the preference of the individual self. To wish to avoid that which you do not like is just another form of preference. Spirit has no preference. It is content, still, at peace. Become, like Me, desireless, without preference, indifferent to "I" and "mine", and you enter the higher Self and find the peace you so desire. Whatever comes, let it come, Arjuna. Whatever goes, let it go. Be unmoved in victory or defeat, triumph or loss, for all is in My hands. All that you will ever experience in this world is Me, Life, guiding you to your final destination. Caught up in the babbling of the ego mind though, overcome with desires and preferences and aversions, all you will ever find is the individual self. Ego, Arjuna, is the enemy of the soul. It blocks you from Me. Beyond the ego, beyond time and space, beyond desire and aversion, I am. Come to Me."

"If you knew what I know about the power of giving, you would not let a single meal pass without sharing it in some way."
-Gautama Buddha

CHAPTER 4

The Path of Knowledge

"Thank you, my good friend," Arjuna said, "for being so kind and patient with me. I am beginning to understand, and to feel the truth of Your words. But I am also confused as to how You have come by this knowledge. You still haven't explained how it is that I come to You in the end. You seem to be hinting that you are some kind of deity. Is this what You are saying?"

"Over the course of our conversation, I will reveal My full identity to you," said Krishna. "As of right now, your human mind cannot yet handle the entirety of what I am—at least not all at once. I mentioned in the beginning of our conversation that I am not who or what you thought Me to be, but much more. Here is another piece to the puzzle of my identity, since you have asked: that which I now teach to you, I have also taught before. I taught it to Surya, who taught it to his son Vaisvastu Manu, who taught it to his son King Iksvaku. For eons this knowledge has been passed down by wise men and philosophers. Eventually, the knowledge was watered down, lost, forgotten. When this occurred, I returned and restored to humanity that which was lost. I have done this many times over the course of human history."

Arjuna balked at Krishna's words. "You taught Surya?"

"I did."

"But Surya existed a hundred billion years ago. How is that even possible?"

THE BHAGAVAD GITA 101

"I am eternal, Arjuna, but from time-to-time I do take on human form, whenever I feel that My presence is needed. Many lives have I lived, as have you—as have we all. But I remember well all of my past incarnations while you do not— you only remember the events of this current lifetime. In fact, I remember all lives ever lived—not just My own, but all."

"If you are eternal," Arjuna asked, "why in the world would You choose to descend into human form? If this existence is the prison, the Hell You say it is, why would You choose to take part?"

"To help you and all of mankind to escape its tethers," Krishna answered. "Whenever the eternal truth, the dharma, the purpose of life begins to falter, begins to fade from the minds of the human race, and humankind begins to lose their way, I return. In every age I have come in order to re-seed the human race with the truth. I have come many times before, in many different forms, and have been given many different names. With each incarnation, holy men flock and listen, they record in scripture what I say and form religions around those sayings in order to preserve My teachings."

"But your teachings are lost over time? Watered down? Forgotten? How can that be?"

"The human mind is tricky. Over a ten-year period, your memory of an event may change several times, often dramatically. Imagine, then, how much a memory could change over the course of a lifetime. Then try to imagine how much more so it could change as a memory or saying is passed from one generation to the next over the course of thousands of years."

"Okay," said Arjuna. "I can see how that could happen. As a child I played a game called 'gossip'. My kindergarten class would form a line and the teacher would whisper something in the first child's ear. Each child would then whisper the message into the next child's ear until the last child was reached. Inevitably, by the time the message reached the final child, it would always be altered quite a bit from the original message. If a message can be altered that much in a simple child's game, I can see just how much more so it would be altered over successive generations."

"Exactly," said Krishna. "This is exactly what happens. Further, instead of focusing on the central core of all my teachings, in all my forms, in all my incarnations, humans choose to fight over the differences between the incarnation their particular religion revolves around and all others. They tend to favor a single incarnation and build a wall of religion around it, believing it to be the one and only teaching to believe in, the one and only Path to righteousness. In order to prove their path correct, they often alter My teachings to fit these needs, to prove their path to be the correct one. This too is the ego at work; the very thing you need to overcome."

"And this is not your intent?" Arjuna asked.

"No, not at all," said Krishna. "But it is understandable, at least to some degree. First of all, the ego is a powerful foe. It is very hard to overcome. Second, with each incarnation, I mold my teachings to match the understandings and needs of the day and age in which I appear, which is confusing to the human mind. The masses get caught up in these differences and miss the core message that is central to all my incarnations. I have no religion, Arjuna. I *am* religion; all of them. You need to dissolve, in your mind, the boundaries that you have erected between the different religions. I did not put them there—humans did. Over time, as I have said, My words have been passed down, and as languages have evolved and taken on newer forms, the meanings of what I have said have become distorted or missed altogether. Yet my central teaching is always the same in every age, it never changes— that you are immortal, and through knowledge and love and selfless actions you may come to know Me and escape the confines of worldly existence. Released from greed and anger and fear, absorbed in the higher Self, you all *can* attain My level of being. This is what I have come once more to teach, for humankind is once again in need of guidance. You are in need of guidance."

"What are the main differences between the teachings of your past incarnations?" Arjuna asked.

"In older cultures, many of My teachings centered around different needs than those of today," Krishna answered. "In certain time periods, for example, people tended to be almost completely materialistic. For them, I taught the need for contemplation of the divine. In later cultures, due to misunderstandings of My previous teachings, holy men would sit in caves all day long and beg for food in their attempts to find Me. I did not mean for them to discard the material world completely, but instead to find a balance that included the spiritual as well as the material. But many later adherents did not understand and began to renounce life entirely. My teachings of that time period, therefore, centered around such a culture, explaining My message in a way that explained the need for participation in human life along

47

with spiritual contemplation. In even later ages, the central misunderstandings of the day were different still. I mold each message around the needs and verbiage of the time period in which I appear."

"Oh, I see," said Arjuna. "But what about the verbiage? The misunderstandings? How does language change Your message over time?"

"If I were you to compare humans to a tree," Krishna said, "in my current incarnation, and tell you that you can tell the merits of a human being by the fruits they bear, just as you can with a fruit-bearing tree, I would mean that you can gauge the maturity level of the Soul in the person before you by their actions. Mature trees produce mature fruit, while immature trees do not. In the same way, humans with minds that have evolved sufficiently perform selfless actions, while humans with minds that have not yet evolved produce selfish actions."

"I am with you so far," said Arjuna.

"In later translations of this current incarnation, the message may change due to alterations in the meaning of the terms I use. For example, the term 'ripe' or 'mature' may eventually be replaced with the term 'bad'. There are no good or bad people, Arjuna, there are only mature Souls and Souls that have not yet matured. This is partly a misunderstanding, a mistranslation of the meaning of ancient words into modern verbiage, and partly an egotistical method of control for people who want their way to be the one and only. It is ironic, Arjuna, that my wish for you all is to overcome your egos and find Me, yet even through my own teachings do humans fight for a way to include ego in the path."

Arjuna ruminated over Krishna's words. "You just said, just a minute ago, that you taught Surya, who taught it to his son Vaisvastu Manu, and so on; you said that you seed the human race with knowledge and that knowledge is passed down through the thinkers and philosophers of each day, yet you tell me not to do so. You tell me to lead only with my actions. Once again, your own words seem to contradict themselves."

"That goes back, once again, to the ego," Krishan explained. "It is your ego, your feeling of self importance, that causes you to desire to teach others. I told you instead to lead with your actions for now because you are not yet free, you have not yet risen above your own ego. What good is it for one prisoner, still held against his will, to instruct another on how to escape? Once free you will become like Me, and only then will you become a fit vessel for the spread of My teachings. Then I will teach through you; we will teach together. For now, you are still in the same prison as those you wish to help, and have no place instructing anyone. Surya reached the ultimate truth, as did Vaisvastu Manu, and so on, which is why they were fit to spread My teachings. Once you have reached the truth for yourself, you too will be fit to spread My message. Until then, I need you to walk the path, to lead by example. Are we clear? Are we ready to go on?"

"I think so," said Arjuna.

"Good. Now I have said that there are two main paths to Eternity: Knowledge and Love. The Path of Love has also been referred to as the Path of Selfless Action. Intellectual, contemplative types like yourself tend to be more suited for the Path of Knowledge, which leads to enlightenment, the direct experiencing of the Soul of the World. For others, the Path of Faith and Devotion, the Path of Selfless Action, the Path of Love seems to work best. But know this: all paths, when followed with the right intent, come to Me. All paths, when done with the right intent, elevate you beyond the self interests of the ego. Though Knowledge and Love are the two main paths humans have found, there are many others, and they are all valid—each person must find his or her own way. It is My doing that each human has a different nature; different talents and different perspectives unique to them and only them. Do not waste your time trying to tell another that their path is incorrect. If they truly seek Me, it is Me they will find, whether they imagine and find Me in personified form, or My truer form which is no form at all."

"Yes, Krishna," Arjuna said. "I understand. And I am beginning to understand Who you claim to be."

"Further, though each Path seems separate, they all cross and merge in the end; they all lead to love and a knowledge of something greater than the self. Using the two main paths as an example, if, through knowledge, you come to see the unity of all life, how could you not find love and feel compelled to help others? Once you come to see Me, you will find nothing but your Self in all others, and nothing in all others but your Self. In doing so, you will realize that I, and only I exist, for I made you in My image—we are of the same Essence. On the other hand, the Path of Faith, the Path of Love, the Path of Devotion and Selfless Action—this path also leads to the same knowledge as you find in the Path of Knowledge. All paths lead to me, Arjuna, *all* paths. Ultimately, they all merge into one. Focus only on your own path and leave the others to

Me. The Path of Knowledge, for which you seem best suited, is long and difficult, steep and full of pitfalls, but it does lead to Self-realization; it does lead to Me in the end. It is the ultimate path, but not the only one. The Path of Love is a bit easier for most people, but also leads to Me as well. Are you still with me?"

"I am." said Arjuna.

"Good," said Krishna. "Then let me go into one more detail. I have already said that no matter the path, action is still required. Even with the Path of Knowledge, action is still mandatory for growth to continue. But not just any action will do—only selfless actions count. The action I am describing has been referred to as 'actionless action', the way of 'no way'. I know this is confusing at your level of conception, so I need to go a little deeper into the subject."

"Please do," said Arjuna.

"The superficial meaning is that actions done for personal gain attaches you more to the ego," Krishna continued. "Actions done by the ego has a "doer", so to speak, and that 'doer' is your lower self, your ego. Actions performed in hopes of reward or the avoidance of suffering serve only yourself and do not raise you above the selfish nature of the ego. At death, you return to the world you are most attached to—in this case the material world. However, actions performed with indifference to reward or punishment, success or failure, victory or defeat disconnects you from the ego, disconnects you from the lower self. Unattached to material results, unattached to material rewards, you have attached yourself to Me, and that is your reward. Even in this life, such a person that lives in this manner walks with Me, and with the death of their body, their consciousness joins mine. Are you with me so far? This idea goes a little deeper ... what comes next is a bit harder to understand."

"I am. I understand," said Arjuna. "Go on."

"I have said that actions performed without attachment to results are performed from the higher Self, from the higher Mind, and is referred to as 'actionless action'. Allow me to explain a bit further why this is: When you rise above the ego, you connect with the higher Self, which, ultimately, is Me. This aligns you, here and now, with the will of the universe. Only actions performed by the ego requires true effort, for you are attempting to go against your inner nature, you are attempting to swim against the Tide of Creation, and cannot be done. The Soul, on the other hand, acts out of its own nature, which is also My nature. What It does is performed effortlessly, for It acts naturally, instinctively, from Its own will, which is also My will. What I do is effortless. What comes forth from Me is simply My nature issuing forth. Though at rest, I achieve all. Without doing a single thing, I leave nothing left undone. When you act out the duties I require of you from the higher Self, you have aligned your duties with my own, and they too become effortless, emanating forth from our combined Essence. When you reach such a state, there is no longer a 'doer' and something that needs to be 'done', for they both become one and the same. The action and the result become one, for I am action and I am the result as well."

"How in the world is that possible?" asked Arjuna. "That makes no sense to me."

"Reach the level of the higher Mind and you will understand," said Krishna. "For now, know that I am the form before you and I am its function. When you perform your duties in the way I have described, it is as if I am the one doing the action through you; I am the doer, I am the action itself, and I am the result of that action. I do not have to work to make the wind blow, or the sun to shine—it is just My nature issuing forth. Enter the flow and all you do will be our combined nature issuing forth. Enter the flow and you become the flow. This concept is as confusing as the idea of eternity to the human mind. In material existence, time is linear. In My realm, all that has ever been or ever will be is all happening at once. There is no loss or gain—all that ever was or will be is right here, now. All who have ever existed are still here, now. Reach the higher mind and the illusions of time and space will fade, and the unity of all things becomes apparent, not simply theoretical constructs and ideas."

"Okay. I think I understand. But are you saying to lose myself in my work? To work for the sake of work, without thought in general?"

"Yes. That is exactly it," said Krishna. " Or at least that is part of it. Do that long enough and you actually enter the flow, become the flow. For now, just know that when you lose yourself in your work, concentrating only on doing your absolute best, releasing all thoughts of outcome, all thoughts of failure or success, your lower mind fades and the higher Mind is able to edge forth—the silent, teeming void of pure potential moves in as the ego mind moves out. Whichever you focus on becomes your reality. Act from your essence and work is almost without action. There is no effort, only your inner nature issuing forth"

"I am beginning to understand," said Arjuna.

"Think of it this way:" Krishna continued. "If you run up a set of stairs by instinct, there is no trouble, and it takes very little effort. But think about the process and your feet get tangled. There is a part of you, deep within that is unborn. It knows—It simply knows. When you hear a rooster crow, do you have to think about it, or do you simply know it is a rooster? If you hear a bird chirping in a far off tree, do you have to think about it, or do you simply know that it is the sound of a bird? This is the Unborn, the Undying within you. It is instinctive, intuitive. Without any training whatsoever, It just knows. The incessant babbling of the ego mind crowds out the subtle, intuitive knowledge of the Unborn."

"I see," said Arjuna.

"Do you ever get ideas out of the blue?" Krishna asked. "This, too, is the Unborn Mind peeking out through the endless chatter of your ego mind. And it usually happens when you are not trying to force an idea—when the ego mind has been exhausted, or when you are asleep. The entire purpose of meditation is to take your focus off the chattering of the ego mind and focus it instead on the silent Void beyond. But you do not have to sit in a room by yourself for hours on end to reach the Unborn, though you may find it helpful, at least in the beginning. No, work done correctly becomes a form of meditation in and of itself. In performing your duties in the way I have outlined, your entire life becomes meditation in action, a holy offering. Every single thing that such a person does becomes spiritual. Unperturbed, indifferent to the storms around you, it is as if you do nothing at all, even when fully emerged and engaged with life."

"Ahhh," said Arjuna. "I do believe I am beginning to understand this concept as well."

"Good," said Krishna, "for most of humankind does not. Most try to entice *Me* to work for *them*. They try to extract rewards out of Me with their own versions of worship and ritual and sacrifice and promises. As I have said, any act of worship performed with good intent does come to Me, but that offering has to come from beyond the ego for it to bear fruit. The only sacrifice I ask is that you sacrifice your life for the better good, in search of Me; to let the higher Self through, to let Me in. The only reward I offer is the eternal reward. No matter the path you choose though, remember that action is needed. Neither the rewards of this world or those of the next can be obtained without action. Actions performed by the ego result in the rewards found in the material world. Actions produced by the higher Mind obtains a far more valuable prize. If no actions are performed, no results can be obtained, worldy or spiritual."

"I get it," said Arjuna. "I understand."

"The battle is yours and yours alone," said Krishna. "You get to *choose* which is more precious to you. You get to *choose* the level of mind you focus on and fight for. Your path, Arjuna, seems to be the Path of Knowledge. It is the ultimate path, for it leads to a direct experience of Me. Even a blatant sinner, or an atheist, or an agnostic can find Me through the Path of Knowledge. Knowledge burns ignorance to ash like nothing else—nothing in this world can withstand its power. Still, no path is wrong. All are dear to Me. All true offerings, in the end, consist of this: outer action with inner renunciation. It is the only thing that lifts you above the ego. Find a way to do this and be content with whatever I send your way or do not send your way and all will be well. Arise now, Arjuna, and continue your journey, for Spirit is obtained only by those who find Me in every form, in every action."

"Out beyond ideas of wrongdoing and rightdoing, there is a field. I will meet you there. When the soul lies down in that grass, the world is too full to talk about. Ideas, language, even the concepts of 'you' and 'me' no longer make any sense."

-Rumi

CHAPTER 5

Renunciation

"You have spoken previously about the Path of Knowledge and the Path of Love. Can you now explain the concepts a bit further?" asked Arjuna. "Specifically, can you please clarify the concept by using concrete examples from everyday life? "

"Of course," said Krishna. "For the Path of Knowledge, let us use the life of a monk as an example. Or the life of a scientist or academician. The Path of Knowledge is a viable path. It is the most direct path, but also the most difficult. The monk renounces the material world by denying him or herself of the life of a husband or wife, the life of a father or mother, and concentrates his or her efforts looking inward. He or she spends a great deal of time in concentration, in learning, in meditation, foregoing many of the pleasantries of this world in hopes of obtaining directly the understanding that leads to liberation. The scientist or academician, likewise, focuses their efforts on the pursuit of knowledge. They, like the monk (but not to the same extreme) forfeit many of the pleasantries of human relations and interactions in their pursuits. The end-product of their efforts is enlightenment—a direct awakening to knowledge. This is the path that most likely suits you best."

"I think so, too," said Arjuna. "But you said before that the way of the monk is wrong. That they are not to renounce life altogether."

"Correct," said Krishna. "There is nothing wrong with inner contemplation, in fact that part is very good. But they still need to *live*. The scientist and academician also spend a lot of time in deep contemplation but still find time to live at least a little bit of their lives outside of their scholastic pursuits. They at least do not live in a cave, secluded from all others."

"I understand," said Arjuna.

"Now let us compare the way of the intellectual to the way of the householder," said Krishna. "Although a monk does not take a family, the scientist or academician may. Still, their main focus is on the accumulation of knowledge, sometimes to the exclusion of true participation in family life. The householder, on the other hand, finds joy and liberation in leading a life centered not around his or her own self-interests, but in taking care of his or her family. It is their main focus, such is their nature. The householder grows to care more for his or her family than they do for their own well-being. Eventually, if the path is followed fully, their love grows and expands to include not only their immediate family, but all living things. The householder, then, is still practicing renunciation, just in a way that is very different from the intellectual. The householder finds liberation not by the accumulation of knowledge, but by forfeiting his or her own personal needs, to a certain extent, for the betterment of his or her family. Through selfless action, the householder finds the Path of Love, the Path of Devotion."

"So both paths involve renunciation, just in different ways?" asked Arjuna. "The intellectual gives up some aspects of the material world and social life in pursuit of knowledge, while the householder renounces his or her own comforts for that of his family."

"Exactly," said Krishna. "And in the end, both paths are the same. Though approached from different angles, each path involves working for something higher than the self. Through contemplation, the monk obtains knowledge that leads to a love for all that is. It is a path that is a bit lonelier in the earlier stages, but that is the nature of those drawn to such a path. Through selfless action, the householder finds love and eventually comes to the same knowledge as the monk. Both find Me, just in their own ways. The monk typically finds me as an impersonal force that animates the living world while the householder tends to find Me in personified form. But both are valid paths—there is no difference to Me. The more progressive minded seem best suited to the path of the monk while the more conservative minded tend to prefer the path of the householder. The as-of-yet ignorant see the two main paths as different, Arjuna, and quabble needlessly over which one is better. But I am telling you, in no uncertain terms, that whoever gives all of his or her soul to either path gains both enlightenment *and* faith, knowledge *and* love."

"I see," said Arjuna, "By renunciation you mean renouncing the ego, moving beyond the self-centered vantage point of the self. But there are different ways to do so, each based on the individual inclination and nature of each person?"

"That is it, Arjuna!" Krishna exclaimed. "The monk, via knowledge, moves beyond the ego level of the mind and finds the higher Mind. Once found, the monk cannot help but concern him or herself with the welfare of all because he or she comes to see the same Soul in all that is. The householder, through love, also moves beyond the level of ego, and concerns him or herself with the welfare of others. Both, in their own way, move beyond the individual desires and passions of the ego self, and in doing so, find Me."

"I understand," said Arjuna.

"Wordly men and women live from the passions of the ego," Krishna added. "They still worship the self and are held captive by its nature. Because they work for the self, they are tied to it. Their actions are performed for material rewards, so they remain rooted in and attached to worldly desires. At death, they return to the earth in search of more material reward. The monk and the true householder, on the other hand, have moved beyond this level of thinking, each in their own way, and perform their duties for the sake of performing them, without regard to personal gain. In the end, they work for something beyond the ego. They work for Me and come to Me in the end. Wherever you set the desire of your heart, that is what you receive; your focus determines your reality. The worldly receive the reward they most cherish, as do the seekers."

"In renouncing the desires of the worldly ego, we are released from its prison?" Arjuna asked.

"Not only that, but by working from and for the Self, all sins are dissolved," Krishna explained.

"Okay, I am confused again," said Arjuna. "Please explain that part further."

"Sin is only known by the ego. The Self knows no such thing," said Krishna. "When working from the ego, there can be error. You can be led astray by the passions and desires of individual gain. When working for the Self though, there can be no error, no sin, for you are working for the All, which knows no error. Dissipate the ego, which is but an illusion anyway, and there is no self for sin to attach to—sin slides off of your Soul like water on a duck. Defeat the ego and you also defeat sin. Defeat the ego and the wheels of karma cease to spin."

THE BHAGAVAD GITA 101

"And then we are liberated, free?" asked Arjuna. "And our reward is in joining you when our bodies pass away?"

"Yes," Krishna answered, "but the rewards reach into this world as well. Here and now, in this existence, renunciation of the self means the end of suffering, the end of turmoil. The one that realizes the Self in all things and all things in the Self lives without fear, without anger, without desire. They live only in love. They live only in knowledge. They have found the All and need nothing else. The reward, you see, is both immediate as well as everlasting. The goal, the purpose of this world, is to find Me *through* all the drama and turmoil and angst. Do so and the struggle is over, both in this world and the one to come."

"I see," said Arjuna.

"I hope you do," said Krishna, "for the way out of the darkness is to let the Light of knowledge, the Light of love through. The darkness does not exist—it is the ego, the great illusion, "the devil", Maya—it is a construct of the human ego. Only the Light exists, and once it enters it burns away all darkness, for darkness cannot remain where the Light exists. Find the Light, either through knowledge or through love, and you will find a peace that never fades or wanes. A peace that can never be lost or taken. The more you let It in, the more It enters; there is no end to Its depths. Find It and you will ride the Tides of Life, content as a wave on the ocean. Without 'doing', without 'effort', you will be carried for the remainder of your days, no matter the storms and dramas that rage all around you. Neither craving nor avoiding, you will have escaped the prison of the ego and found everlasting peace. You must still act though, you must still live, but the actions will be done through you, not by you."

"So, you are saying that up to now, I have been attached to the individual desires of the ego," asked Arjuna, "swimming against the Tide of the Universe? But if I find the higher Mind, I join It's flow and enjoy the ride?"

"Yes," said Krishna. "I do believe you are getting it. Do so, and in all that you do from that moment forth, whether it be eating or drinking, sleeping or breathing or working, you will realize that all is Spirit will working through you. Then you will say, 'I do nothing at all; it is all done through me.' Try with all your might to find such peace in the pleasantries of this world though and (as you yourself have come to find) your efforts will be both exhausting and futile. Learn instead to endure the storms of life and you will be transformed by them—you will pass beyond them. You will then find a peace that is not transient but enduring, a peace that surpasses all human understanding. This is the only error of the monk, as we have discussed. Many monks attempt to avoid life altogether. In doing so they avoid the very lessons that will eventually carry them forward in their progress."

"I understand," said Arjuna. "The way of the monk, in and of itself, is not in error, as long as life itself is not completely avoided."

"Yes," said Krishna, "That is it. The path to Nirvana, the path to Heaven is found by living life, not by avoiding it entirely. Seek it there and you will eventually find Me in all that you see before you and within you as well. I am all forms, Arjuna, yet I have no form. I am everywhere, I am everything ... I am All. Find Me and there is nowhere you will be able to look (inward or outward) that I am not. I am human, I am animal, I am plant, I am stone ... and I am Consciousness

Itself. I am that which sees and also that which is seen. I am that which is thought and that which thinks. I am sinner and saint, democrat and republican, male and female; yet I am more—I am the unity between such limited opposites. I am all that is as One. Come to know Me and find My peace, which you may then take as your own."

"Such a peace I have never found, never known!" Arjuna exclaimed. "I am now finding that peace to be my one and only desire."

"As it should be," said Krishna. "This very change in your desire proves that you are showing progress. You have found material existence empty and begun to value something far more precious. What you seek has been before you all along, waiting to be discovered. Now that you are ready, I have come to lead you to It. And all I am doing is reminding you of who and what you are, as well as what you are here to do. Remain within the Center, calmly detached from all results and you will find the Self, which dwells eternally at ease. Reclaim your birthright, Arjuna—that is the task I place before you, the only duty I ask of you. Realize and become the Watcher within, simply observing as life swirls and rolls and rails about you and within your mind. The things of this world cannot be depended on—the matured find in them no lasting joy. Learn to focus your mind instead on the eternal and you will find that freedom is nearer than near. I am already here, Arjuna, wating."

"Yes," said Arjuna. "I am compelled to continue to fight! What you have described is the very thing I seek. I was just looking in all the wrong places."

"What you most want is what I want for you as well," said Krishna. "Our wills are aligned, you just have to realize it for yourself. But in your journey, remember this at all times: there is no good or bad, only those that are ready and those that are not-yet-ready. Those that you call bad are but ignorant. They are to be helped, not scorned or hated. They do not yet understand, though they will with time. They fight a battle within that you know nothing of. I do know of their battles, and I assure you that if you understood, you would forgive them as I do. You fought a similar battle, did you not?"

"I did," Arjuna admitted.

"The battles that rage within them come forth in their actions and decisions," Krishna went on "They are scared and angry and confused—that is their only true sin, born of their ignorance of the truth. Lead them, Arjuna, with your actions for now, and once you yourself have escaped, you will be able to do even more. Renounce the religion of the ego as is followed by the masses and follow instead the religion of the Soul."

"Are you here, before me, or are you within My mind? For I now find that I cannot tell the difference," asked Arjuna.

"As you wish, Arjuna—that is how I appear. For you, I appear as the higher Mind issuing forth. For others, I appear in personified form—I instruct through more material means."

"In the end, it makes no difference?" asked Arjuna.

"None whatsoever," Krishna answered.

"Be kind to all that exists. This is true religion."
-The Buddha

CHAPTER 6

Mastering the Mind

"We have gone into depth on a few subjects, Arjuna, and I sense that you are beginning to catch on."

"I think I am," Arjuna admitted.

"Good. Then I would like to move on to a more advanced subject—it is time for you to learn a few specific tools that will help to ensure success on your quest. You are an intellectual type, Arjuna, and I believe the Path of Knowledge to be the path you are most suited for."

"Again," said Arjuna, "I believe I agree with you."

"Then I would like to teach you now about the science of Self-Knowledge, the science of Self-Realization. As I told you before, the Path of Knowledge is a valid path, but it is difficult—the learning curve is steep. It involves a deep understanding and mastery of the mind, which is no easy feat, I can assure you. This is why the masses tend to prefer the Path of Love, the Path of Faith. What I wish to do now is to outline the difficulties of the Path of Knowledge as well as the procedures by which you may obtain victory. The end result of what I am about to teach you is a direct experience with the divine, an 'awakening' to the truth of the universe. I must warn you though that when such a thing happens, it is powerful beyond anything that you can now imagine. Everything changes before you, yet at the same time, absolutely nothing is different."

"Everything changes, yet nothing is different?" Arjuna asked. "Please go into a little more detail on this point. I definitely do not understand."

"Awakening is an experience that is beyond human conception," said Krishna. "Something that is better experienced than explained. Still, I will try to give you an idea of the experience … It is like a child that learns that Santa Claus is not real after believing in him for many years. For that child, his or her entire world changes, though in fact, nothing has really changed. The only real difference is in perception, the lack of a belief in the existence of something that never really existed in the first place. Still, it alters the child's perception of the world, the way he or she thinks the world works, and such a change is … life altering."

"Okay," Arjuna said. "I think I understand. You see the same world, but it takes on a new meaning. Is that correct? You see the same world before you, but understand it differently?"

"Correct," Krishna answered. "In the case of Santa Claus, finding out that he does not exist makes the world seem less magical. Enlightenment works in the exact opposite manner. Truly see this world for what it is and you will know magic beyond your wildest dreams. Not the sleight-of-hand magic of conjurers and entertainers but real magic—the indescribable miracle of a living and conscious Intelligence that moves within all that exists. Awaken to this Presence and the world around you will look the same as it did before to your earthly eyes, but you will no longer be perceiving this world through those earthly eyes alone. You will also be viewing this world through an inner vision and an inner understanding that perceives and comprehends far more than your earthly eyes and your earthly mind ever could."

"So my perception and therefore my understanding of this world will change?" asked Arjuna.

"Yes. And as your perception changes, as your understanding deepens, so too does your experience of this world. It will be as if you have been reborn from this current world of yours into another that is exactly the same, yet also profoundly different. Such a change in perception is why the enlightened are no longer tempted by gold and silver and jewels. They have awakened to the miracle beyond the form and have fallen in love with It. For such a person, a bar of gold or a diamond is no more precious than a pebble or a handful of sand, for that person now perceives the living Force vibrating Itself into existence as the forms they see before them. The awakened fall in love with the miracle and lose their fascination with the form."

"I see," said Arjuna. "They now live within a new reality—the same reality as before, yet also very different—all due to a shift in their perception? A shift in their focus?"

"Yes, Arjuna, that is it. Perceiving their own immortal nature as fact, they begin to see that same nature everywhere, in all that exists, and no longer find danger or discomfort in any situation. They begin to perceive Spirit, Consciousness in all forms of life, whether it be precious or plain, plant or animal, sinner or saint, democrat or republican, male or female. Beyond the form before them, in their mind's eye, the enlightened intuit Me, the unified Source beyond the duality of this world, and come to see That as the ultimate reality. I become their focus, their treasure, and they desire Me beyond all else. See this but once, my good friend, and you will not be able to help but feel the same way."

"I very much wish this for myself," said Arjuna. "Please keep instructing me, I am listening!"

"The awakened also come to know intimately the role played by their own mind in creating the perception of the world they see before them. Perception is everything, Arjuna. Change your mind and you change your world! Come to know thyself and you will know all, for I, the Self, and the miracle of life are of the same cloth."

"But … to get to such a realization I must master my mind?" asked Arjuna. "How is that even possible? The mind is a wanderer. It flits to and fro all day long, and it takes me with it wherever it goes. Whatever thought it puts forth I am drawn into. Whatever mood it adopts becomes my own. I have tried many times to calm it but have failed each time. The mind seems to me as if it were actually a chariot driven by monkeys that have been stung by a scorpion—the idea of taming it seems impossible!"

"You feel this way because you haven't yet begun to understand the puzzle that is the mind," Krishna responded. "To solve the puzzle you must first understand the mind and how it works. Then and only then will you be able to plan an escape route out of its maze. It is difficult though, as you say—the ego mind is a powerful foe!"

"Then let us push on! I am up for the task!"

"Good. The main tool I will teach you to use will be meditation. I know you have tried it before …"

"I have …"

"But now I will guide you. I will show you the way. Whether you call it meditation, deep concentration, single pointed focus, prayer ... it does not matter. Arguing over the title you give it is merely more ego-squabbling by the uninformed. Call it what you will, but it is all the study of the mind and how to overcome it. The ego mind will always guide you back to captivity within its prison if you allow it, yet that is no longer an option for you."

"I understand and agree. I cannot go back to the world that I knew before. I am ready to advance. Please go on ..."

"The first step, as I have said, is to study the mind. You must see for yourself how it works in all of its guises and temptations. To do so you must begin by finding a quiet, comfortable area to practice. Eventually, when your focus is strong enough, you will need to take this training into your everyday world. But your power of focus is too weak right now, so you must begin in an area that has as few distractions as possible. Like any other muscle, the muscle of focus needs to be built up slowly at first. Try to use it from the beginning in the real world with all its storms, and dramas, and dilemmas and you will most likely fail. You will get frustrated and quit."

"Okay," said Arjuna. "I am with you. Please continue."

"Good. Then find a quiet, comfortable spot, Arjuna, and simply sit."

"Sit? That is all?" asked Arjuna.

"Sit and watch," Krishna answered. You failed in your meditations before because you tried to *control* the mind. You tried to calm it, yet this cannot be done. Give the ego mind your focus and it will run away with you. Instead, simply observe your mind in action. Study the enemy for now. Watch how it runs this way and that. How it comes up with ideas and desires and chores and emergencies and tasks, all without your doing. See how it demands you get up and do this or that, how it demands you pay attention to it. If it is anxious, it demands you to be anxious as well. Watch. That is all. You need to *understand* the enemy before you will be able to defeat it."

"Just watch?" asked Arjuna. "I think I understand, but still ..."

"By just watching, Arjuna, you will come to see that you are not in control of the ego mind. It is not you, though you have taken it to be, which is why it has controlled you until now. It has been in charge, Arjuna, but no more. Focus functions very similarly to breathing: it is an automated process, but one that can also be directed intentionally. First though, you must see the ego mind for what it is; an automated tool that is not who or what you are. You *can* stand aside and look at your thoughts without entering them—and you must. You cannot control the ego mind, but you can control where you place your focus. Resist not its babblings, Arjuna, but instead separate yourself from them. If you can separate your attention from your thoughts, what does that tell you?"

"That they are not who I am? That I am not actively, intentionally creating them?" Arjuna answered.

"Correct," said Krishna. "The ego mind is but a tool of this existence, no different than any other bodily function. By standing aside and watching the flow of thoughts, you have separated yourself from the ego mind's meanderings, proving that they are not you, or products of your creation. Standing aside, you can choose the vantage point of the Watcher, the

Observer, the Self, simply allowing all ego thoughts to rise and then fall away of their own accord."

"Then why do I even have an ego mind? What is its use?" Arjuna asked.

"The ego mind is a tool for the material world, just like your arms, your legs, your vision, or your hearing. And it serves a dual purpose. You do need it, at least in the beginning, for it is a tool to keep you safe; it tells you not to pick up snakes, not to leap off cliffs, that kind of thing. But it also serves as a prison to keep you in this world until you have matured beyond it. Step out of its flow and you begin living as the Observer, the Watcher, the Self, not the ego. You can still heed the ego mind's warnings when applicable, but you can now *choose* when to heed the warnings and ideas of the ego mind and when to ignore them. Do this and the mind becomes what it was designed to be—merely a tool for your use in navigating this world, not your master. Observation of the mind, Arjuna, is the first step to awakening. It both shows the problem and begins to deliver you from it at the same time."

"It seems as if You are telling me to drift away from all I have ever known," said Arjuna. The idea frightens me more than I can say. I feel like I would be lost. In fact, I feel lost now."

"And lost you will be, at least for a time," Krishna responded. "It shows that you are on the right path. You have to be lost to this world in order to find the places that can't be found within it. Do not worry. It won't be long before another shore will come into view. Just endure the fear for now and trust in Me."

"How fast does it happen?" Arjuna asked. "How long will I feel lost? It seems such a very difficult and a very frightening thing to do, but if I am able to achieve it, how long before I reach the far shore?"

"At first, your ventures beyond the ego mind will not last long. It will pull you back into its reality over and over and over. With practice, your level of focus will become stronger and stronger until eventually you will be able to pry your focus away from its hold at will. The longer you are able to remain detached from the ego mind the more you will find yourself operating from a higher level of consciousness, a higher level of understanding. Eventually, you may fully become the Watcher and begin to adopt the vantage point of the higher Self in all that you do. The process is gradual for most people, yet it is why you are here. The mental muscle must be exercised. For now it is very weak. But do the work and you will eventually come to realize who and what you are. Reach this point and the destination is at hand. The path may seem scary at first, especially when you first dare to stray from the ego, which is all you have known, but that will not last long. Exactly how long I cannot say. The journey is different for each person."

"After the fear? Then what?" asked Arjuna.

"Then it feels like coming home."

"And if I don't get there in this lifetime?"

"As I said before, you try again in your next incarnation. But no progress is ever lost. No effort is ever in vain. You begin the next life from whatever level you are able to achieve within this one."

"But I am already the Watcher?" asked Arjuna, confused.

"Yes, you already *are* the Watcher, but you have to come to realize this for yourself," Krishna explained. "This is the great trick of the ego, and the secret to your captivity. What you seek is already yours, but the ego keeps it from you. It clouds the realization of your true identity as dust distorts your reflection from a mirror. Escape the maze of the ego mind and your true identity becomes apparent. You are immortal, Arjuna. Practice as I have taught and you will know this beyond a shadow of doubt. For now, it is still only a platitude—a nice teaching that you hope to be true."

"You said this is the first step in meditation. Is there a second?" Arjuna asked.

"There is. To detach yourself further from the constant babbling of the ego mind, begin attempting to increase the power of your focus away from its pull. This is where the mental muscles really begin to grow. Like any other muscle, the mental muscle only grows with use, so use it on a regular basis and it will respond. As you meditate, begin focusing your attention on anything other than your thoughts: the tip of your nose, the area between your eyebrows, your breath, a sound ... anything. As you do, you will discover just how weak the power of your focus really is, for the ego mind will pull you back into its reality over and over and over again. Each time you realize this has occurred, calmly return your focus back to the object you have chosen as your focal point."

"And what will this do?" Arjuna asked.

"First," said Krishna, "you will once again see, even more deeply now, just how hard it is to escape the pull of the ego mind. The second thing that will happen is that you will begin to spend more and more time outside the realm of the ego's reality, and begin to discern the existence of a quietude, a peace that is free from sorrow, free from despair, free of the turmoils and dilemmas of life. You will begin to tap into a higher level of Mind, and you can begin to choose to intentionally take shelter in its grace. The ego mind will still be a tool from which you may choose when necessary, but your higher Mind will start to become the default level from which you operate. Do this often enough and it will become habit. Life will still storm and rage all around you, but you will begin to be able, at will, to separate yourself from its torrential currents and choose the still, wise waters of the Self. The ego mind will eventually begin to fade into background noise as you rest more and more in the peace of the Self. The longer you do so, the more the Self expands until you understand that It is all that exists, both in this world and the world beyond. Reach this state and you will be like a candle sheltered from the wind that does not flicker in the slightest, even during the most violent of storms. Are you still with Me?"

"I think so," Arjuna muttered.

"The ego is a filter, Arjuna, the great deceiver, the great interpreter through which you perceive and experience this world. You do not see this world as it is, but as you are. All of your experiences are filtered through your ego, which gives this world all the meaning it has for you. Rise above the ego, separate yourself from its filter, and you see the world directly, objectively, as it really is, not subjectively, as the ego describes it to you. You become like an eagle, viewing the ongoings of this world from far above, out of reach of all that is going on below. Are you still with Me? There is one last step. Are you ready for it?"

"I think I am."

"The final step is to take this state of mind out into the real world; to begin practicing not in solitude but in the hectic torrent that is daily life. Life becomes your teacher, life becomes your test, forcing you deeper and deeper into the Self. As you become increasingly able to remain detached from the ego mind, even during the most turbulent of storms, the peace and contentment you so desire will grow to a crescendo. Detached from the storms, Spirit will come more and more into view. It will become your focus, what you live by. Only then will you be whole. Only then will you be free. The higher Self, Arjuna, is the only true friend that you have. The lower self is the only true enemy. The war you face is an inner war, my friend. It is the battle that you are here to fight. You are fighting your way beyond your ego. You are fighting your way to Me."

"My brain is only a receiver. In the Universe, there is a core from which we obtain knowledge, strength and inspiration. I have not penetrated into the secrets of this core, but I know that it exists."
-Nikola Tesla

CHAPTER 7

Absolute Reality

"Listen closely, Arjuna, for there is more to learn in order to prepare you for the successful outcome of your journey."

"Okay," said Arjuna. "I am ready."

"I have said that the reality of the ego is subjective, but that there is an objective reality that exists beyond the filter of the individual ego. I have given you several tools to see this for yourself."

"Meditation and non-attachment are the main ones, correct?"

"Correct. Once you have mastered those, you will have no more need for My guidance. For now, I'd like to instruct you further."

"Please do."

"The material world before you is illusory, yet extremely difficult to overcome. The ego mind plays a role in this treachery, as I have previously outlined. Bypass the ego and your perception changes. You begin to see things as they actually are, not as your ego interprets them for you."

"And as my perception changes, so does my world?" asked Arjuna.

"Precisely. I would now like to attempt to explain what it is that you can expect when you awaken to Absolute, Objective Reality. Explanations are poor replacements of the actual experience, but I do want to try and prepare you for what is to come. Awakening may come as quite a shock otherwise."

"Go on," said Arjuna.

"When you awaken," Krishna continued, "you will come to see yourself for who and what you are. And you will come to see Me for Who and What I am."

"And What are You?" Arjuna asked, a bit tentatively.

"I am the Light within all. In fact, I am All. From Myself did all come forth, and unto Me do all return. 'Split a piece of wood, I am there. Lift up a stone and you will find Me.' I am earth, Arjuna, and I am fire and water. I am air and I am ether. I am grass and dirt and metal. I am the breath in your lungs, the blood in your arteries, the rhythmic thrum of your heart. I am the cells of your flesh and the hum of your voice. I am the planets and the stars and all the space between. I am the mind, Consciousness Itself. I am reason. I am intellect. I am the invisible Spirit, the foundation, the creator and mover of life. I am life Itself, both the substance from which life emerges and the animator of that substance as well. I am solar systems and universes and dimensions, and I am the intelligence that holds them all together. I am gravity. I am the law of attraction. I am the beginning and the end, the womb of existence. There is nothing more fundamental or primal than I. All worlds, all dimensions, all beings are strung together like pearls on a single thread. I am each pearl on that thread and I am also the thread itself, as well as the creator and controller of the thread. I am the taste in water, the light and warmth of the sun, the glow of the moon. I am the sacred OM, the vibratory sound of creation. I am the manliness of the male, the femininity of the female, and the attraction between the two. I am sex and desire and lust and reproduction. I am love. I am the fragrance of the earth and the brilliance of light. I am the laugh of an infant, the purr of a lover, and the cry of the dying. I am the intelligence of the wise, the beauty of the appealing, and the strength of the strong. I am the primordial source of creation, the Splendor of Existence. I am the Soul of the World, the eternal germ of reality. I am all that is, both in this world and in all others, which number far more than all the grains of sand upon the earth. Beyond even this, I am. Awaken, Arjuna, and all you will find in any direction will be Me."

"And what am I?" asked Arjuna.

"The same as I, for I made you in My image. You are a sacred piece of the Whole, yet at the same time, the Whole in a single sacred piece."

"I do not yet understand how that can be," Arjuna admitted. "It seems beyond comprehension."

"It is," Krishna confirmed, "but only for a short while longer. Awaken and all will be known. For now, it is still only a teaching, but one that you are ready for. It took a long time for you to reach this point, Arjuna. For eons you were like those around you, led only by the senses, ignorant of the inner vision that sees perfectly. Like the others, you were ensnared by the illusory shadows of reality. You lived *within* those shadows and *for* those shadows, ignorant of the truth from which those shadows are cast. But you have now made it to the edge of reality. The illusory nature of this world is nearly insurmountable, yet you found your way clear, and are on the cusp of all that you have hoped for. Unlike those around you, you have begun to intuit My presence in all that is. I tell you this now to restate that there is no evil, Arjuna, only ignorance. You were not evil in your past lives, only ignorant. You erred, you sinned, but only because you could not see the truth. Remember this at all times when dealing with those who are still trapped in the prison of the self. Reserve your judgment of them, for you *were* them. All that they do now you have also done before, at some point or other. To judge another is to judge yourself. Do you understand?"

"I do," said Arjuna.

"The journey is long and difficult," Krishna continued. "Everywhere you look, there is suffering. There is no need to add to it, Arjuna. The pull of the ego is hard to surpass, so be kind and gentle to all you meet."

"I will."

"In the end, all get what they ask for. Those that ask for attachment to the material world receive it, and return to it over and over again, until they eventually grow weary of it, just as you have. And those who ask to surpass it find Me, and at death come to Me. All who truly seek will find, so choose well what you seek. Those who seek Me will love Me as I love them. Yet My love cannot reach those who do not reach for Me. Such a person is in Hell, Arjuna. Be kind. They have walled themselves off from Me, and know only darkness."

"I understand," said Arjuna.

"Truly understand, and you will say 'God is All'. Yet you will not just say it, you will know it. You will *live* it. Those that are trapped in illusion, they are their own gods. They follow the ego's direction. Yet, if a person is good, and acts in goodness, even if they are still ignorant of my presence, they are progressing. All that is good, if earnestly given, finds its way to Me. If another, Arjuna, is on a good path, though not one you recognize, leave them be, for I choose to receive them, and it is My choice not yours. Conversely, if a person prays to Me and sings hymns in My name and thinks he or she serves Me, yet their deeds and actions speak otherwise, in truth, they still worship their own ego. Their offerings do not reach Me but return to them. Fleeting are the treasures of the material world, Arjuna. The wise come to value them not. Are you still with Me."

"Always," Arjuna answered. "Please continue."

"I know all that ever was, is, or will be. I know all that has ever been said or done—all that will ever be said or done. Yet I myself am beyond human comprehension. Try to define Me, it cannot be done. Try to name Me, and you will fail. Speak for Me and you will be wrong—My motives are beyond your own. Unnamable, formless yet all forms, I am the Root of existence. Intuit the truth that lies just beyond human conception and you have a chance to understand."

"Now you speak in riddles!" Arjuna complained.

"I am the Unity from which the world of duality was formed, Arjuna. I am beyond human conception. The only way to express My nature *is* in parables and riddles. Intellect cannot reach Me, only imagination."

"I think I am beginning to get a sense of that as well," Arjuna admitted.

"In the beginning there was naught but Me, the One. From the One was born the two, the division that creates, defines and drives the material world—the male and the female, the proton and the electron, the positive and the negative. This duality is the reality of the material world. It is what creates it, drives it. Yet Unity is its source. All beings are born into the dualistic world of division and illusion which leads them into isolation and fear, desire and aversion, anger and hate.

Duality is the trap, the root of all ignorance, the source of all suffering. And it is driven by ego, sustained by ego. Transcend the ego and you transcend duality. Take refuge in Me, Arjuna. Attain the ultimate freedom. Let the isolation and loneliness of duality fade into the illusion that it is. Within the Unity all sins are shed and you will come to know 'Brahman' the Father. You will come to know 'Atman' the Son, and 'Karma' the Holy Spirit. You will intuit all that now eludes you. You will understand how all that I have said works together in the singular, glorious, and miraculous mechanism of existence. More precious than any holy book in print, you will have discovered the truth, and the truth will set you free. You will have found Heaven, both here on earth, and beyond this existence as well."

"Where is the Door to God? In the sound of a dog barking.
In the ring of a hammer. In a drop of rain. In the face of
Everyone I see."
- Hafiz (Sufi poet)

CHAPTER 8

Salvation

"Brahman, the Father?" Arjuna asked. "Atman the Son, and Karma the Holy Spirit? What are these things? Please instruct me further. It sounds like I have even more to learn."

"Most of what I am now going to elaborate on I have said before—I want to instruct you further on the mechanism of salvation. However, there *are* a few new concepts that I need to put forth first."

"Please do," said Arjuna.

"Existence," Krishna continued, "is born of a Trinity—a Triunity; three seemingly separate entities that are, in the end, actually a single, non-separate Entity. This concept is found, in various forms, in most of the major religions. I am the Father, Brahman, the Supreme Creator, the Soul of the Universe. Call me the Mother if you wish, for there is no name or concept that can contain or describe Me. I am neither male nor female, human or otherwise, yet in order to converse, I must be referred to in some manner. Father is as good a name as any, and somewhat appropriate, for all that exists are but My offspring."

"I see," said Arjuna.

"The Atman, also known as the Son (or the Daughter if you prefer), is the individual soul that enters into and gives consciousness to each life form. It is but a morsel of Spirit existing in material form—an individualized portion of the Whole. Yet the Entirety, the Whole of My essence, is reflected within each individual part, within each individual soul. I know your human mind cannot yet grasp this concept, Arjuna, but begin to accustom yourself to the idea."

"I am trying," Arjuna responded.

"Karma, the Holy Spirit, is the animating force of life. It is the aspect of My being that spurs all that is into continual motion. It is as if the battery pack of the universe. Atoms combine and swirl, materials are formed, solar systems spin, and universes evolve. The Holy Spirit is the impetus for all of this. It encompasses the laws of life that govern and drive existence with unerring precision, including the cyclical nature of death and rebirth."

"But, you said that you are One. A Unified Whole," Arjuna argued. "It now seems as if you are saying something completely different."

"The human mind cannot conceive of what I am, Arjuna. Sometimes it is easier to break My being into parts in order to be better understood. But yes, you are correct; I am One. All is Me."

"Okay. So You are all three, combined into One? Is that what you are saying?"

Krishna nodded. "I as the Father exist in the world of Spirit. I as the Son exist within each being in the material world. I as the Holy Spirit create and animate the outer world of form. Most people have a very difficult time comprehending this— that there is but One, yet It simultaneously exists in several forms, in multiple worlds, carrying out an infinite number of duties. They believe there must be more than One doing all of this, which is why so many religions break me down into multiple gods. Yet there is only One. The Trinity is Me, and all the gods combined is Me as well. I am omnipresent, I am All. The Trinity is but a tool that may allow you to better understand how One can do and be so many different things, all at once."

"I see your point," Arjuna admitted. "It does make it easier. But in the end, You are just describing three different aspects of Yourself? Three different divisions that are actually not divisions, only different aspects of Your being?'

"Precisely" Krishna answered. "Now I would like to elaborate on salvation and the mechanism by which it is obtained. I know we have touched on this topic several times already, but I would like to go a little bit deeper into the subject."

"Please do," said Arjuna.

"The world you see before you is actually energy (and ultimately the Holy Spirit) vibrating at different rates and frequencies and modes. Every form, every object you see in this world has a unique vibrational pattern which causes atoms to line up in a manner specific to the form you see before you. This is difficult to understand. Are you with Me so far?"

"I think so," said Arjuna. "Matter is made up of energy. Though it seems solid to our senses, in the end, it is all just the same energy vibrating at different speeds, thereby forming different patterns. The differences in speed and pattern determines the material form the energy assumes."

"That is correct," said Krishna. "This not only explains individual phenomena, but also entire realms. The energy of the material world vibrates slowly. As a result, the material world seems very solid, very dense. The Spiritual realm, on the other hand, vibrates at a much higher rate, and so has no density, no solidity to it whatsoever. Are you still with Me? "

"It is hard for me to accept," Arjuna admitted, "but yes, I do understand what you are saying."

"Both realms," Krishna went on, "being made of energy, can neither be created nor destroyed (as your laws of physics have proclaimed), but can only change from one form to another. You, Arjuna, are not your body, nor are you your ego mind. Instead, you are the same energy, the same Spirit that created the material world, vibrating at a frequency and pattern unique only to you, giving you an earthly form and an earthly consciousness that is different from all others. This energy, not your ego mind or earthly flesh, is your true nature. As such, you can neither be created nor destroyed, but can only change form."

"What about my body and my ego mind?" Arjuna asked. "What happens to them?"

"They are mortal. Both can, and eventually will, be destroyed," Krishna answered. "Actually, destroyed is the wrong term. They too are immortal and cannot be destroyed, but go on to create other life forms. But as they are not part of you, they do not go with you as your consciousness moves on, which is why I referred to them as mortal. You do not get to keep them."

"But I go on, for I am not my body or my ego mind?" Arjuna asked.

"Correct," said Krishna. "So let us move on to the concept of consciousness. Consciousness, like matter, also vibrates at different levels of frequency. Humans are born with a very low level of consciousness. Ultimately, what this means is that you begin your human existence living from the lowest level of your earthly mind—the subconscious level. The subconscious mind vibrates at a very low frequency. It is that aspect of your earthly mind that promotes knee-jerk responses to life. It is designed to keep you safe. It is your instinct, and it tells you that you need to eat, that you need to procure the necessary means of survival, that you do not need to be picking up snakes or jumping off cliffs ..."

"Like the ego mind."

"Exactly. The subconscious mind is the ego-centric portion of the mind that keeps you safe in the early years of your existence—the years before you begin to consciously understand this world—and it makes up a substantial portion of the ego mind. It is there for a reason, but it is also the mental level that tells you that your needs need to be met above all others'—that you need to be suspicious of all others, that you are in competition with all others. It is the level of mind that tells you that survival is a zero-sum game—that survival is you versus all others. The subconscious mind isolates you, walls you off from everyone else, including Me. As important as it is in the beginning, the ego mind becomes a barrier to progress as you go on. It promotes feelings of separation, which leads to the emotions of selfishness and anger, fear and divisiveness."

"So, the subconscious mind is about me. About my survival. About me and me alone?" Arjuna asked.

"Yes. Exactly," said Krishna. "But as you age and gain experience, your conscious mind begins learning the rules and ropes of this world. As it does so, it grows and expands and matures and begins to take the reins, Arjuna. It begins to take over. As it does, it pushes the ego-centric subconscious mind further and further into the background. Instead of reacting mindlessly to the turmoils and tribulations of life, the conscious mind allows you to begin *choosing* your own responses. The conscious mind operates at a much higher level of vibration than the subconscious mind. With higher levels of vibration come higher levels of perception. You become aware that the subconscious mind does not always promote the most appropriate, most beneficial reactions. You become aware that all dilemmas in life do not have to be you versus others. You become cognizant of other solutions, solutions that span beyond the 'me only' ideology of the unripened mind. You can begin choosing these solutions over the knee-jerk reactions of the subconscious mind. This evolution of consciousness is the entire reason you are here. It is the ultimate purpose of your sojourn in the material realm. You are here for the expansion of your mind, the expansion of your consciousness, and therefore the expansion of your perception. You are here to break free of the prison of the 'Bad Place' that you are in and find the liberation of the 'Good Place'. All of this occurs with the maturing of human consciousness"

"So, growing in consciousness is the purpose of this existence, or at least one of them?" asked Arjuna. "And even if we are not actually aware of it, or intentionally seeking it, it occurs anyway, naturally, over the course of our lives?"

"You are correct, Arjuna. On both accounts. As you age, and as your learning and understanding of this world grows, you outgrow your slavery to the subconcious mind and enter the conscious level. As you continue to grow, your conscious mind continues to expand into higher and higher levels of comprehension, into higher and higher levels of perception. Once again, all of this is the result of vibration. As the conscious mind matures, it begins to operate from a higher level of vibrational frequency."

"Can you give an example of the mind expanding into higher levels of comprehension?" Arjuna asked.

"Of course. As a child you operated from the subconscious level of the mind alone. All was about you and your world and your comfort. It was all you knew. You believed in Santa Claus and the Easter Bunny because they were magical genies that provided you with things that you desired. But you eventually outgrew this belief. As your consciousness expanded, your perception of the world outgrew the ability to believe in Santa Claus and the Easter Bunny. It outgrew these beliefs and delivered you into a new reality. One in which these things could not exist."

"I see. Can you go on?" asked Arjuna. "Can you show how consciousness continues to expand throughout life?"

"Of course. You eventually outgrew the childish mind and matured into a teenager. Though no longer believing in Santa Claus and the Easter Bunny, your perception was still mostly ego-centric. All was still about you and only you, about your needs and what was best for you. Further, your beliefs and only your beliefs were correct. But you eventually outgrew this as well. As you matured into adulthood, your focus expanded beyond yourself alone and into a concern and compassion for your spouse, your children, and your friends. As you continued to age, your focus began to extend outward beyond even these things, encompassing a wider and wider group of concerns. You came to care about poverty and starvation in other nations, in other peoples; even those that have other skin colors, follow other political systems, speak other languages, or practice other religions. If you mature enough in a lifetime, your compassion extends to all of life. This is true love, complete love. Are you still with Me, Arjuna?"

"I am."

"What I have just described," Krishna went on, "is the natural progression of human consciousness. As you live, your conscious mind matures, whether you are aware of it or not. As it matures, it begins to vibrate at higher and higher rates, increasing your power of perception and therefore compassion, until you eventually outgrow the conscious mind as well, just as you did with the subconscious mind. This is the level that you have come to. You are on the cusp of transitioning from your conscious mind to the next level of perception. A perception that extends beyond this world alone. A perception that extends beyond the understanding of the subconscious and conscious minds."

"Okay," said Arjuna. "I think I get it. So evolution beyond the ego mind is the natural state of humankind, but it takes time."

"That is it, Arjuna! But each person grows at their own pace. There are adults, even seniors who are still operating from the subconscious mind and lower levels of the conscious mind. They still care only for themselves and maybe a friend or family member or two. They still believe that their opinions and views are the only valid ones. It is okay, though. They will be reborn and get to try again. They get as many attempts as it takes for their consciousness to mature beyond the lower levels of mind and into the highest levels. Just as fruit ripens on the branch, so too do humans ripen on the limbs of the material world. It makes no difference if you are spiritual, religious, or even agnostic or atheistic in your views, this is the natural progression. It occurs in you all."

"So even atheists and agnostics progress?" Arjuna asked.

"Absolutely. They just do it in their own way. They may call Me science or knowledge, but it makes no difference to Me. Each conceives of Me and pursues Me in his or her own way."

"Which is why all paths, if earnestly traveled, are valid?" asked Arjuna.

"Correct," Krishna answered. "There is one more concept I need to go into before I can tie all of this together. Are you ready?"

"I think I am."

"Life is cyclical. There is a morning, a noon, an afternoon, and a night, correct?" Krishna asked.

"Correct," Arjuna answered.

"And there is a winter, a spring, a summer and a fall. Correct?"

"Correct."

"These are but the cycles of life. The works of Me. The works of Karma, the Holy Spirit. All of life goes through these cycles. The planets go through these cycles. Solar systems and universes go through these cycles. Suns go through these cycles. Dimensions go through these cycles. And all life forms go through these cycles. You know them as birth, adulthood, middle age, and death."

"I am with you."

"Just as the earth goes through a spring, a summer, a fall, and the death of winter, followed by another spring, so too do humans go through these same cycles of birth, growth, decline and death, followed by rebirth as well. By the laws of Karma, by the laws of the Holy Spirit, *where* you are reborn depends on your level of consciousness at death. If at the end of the existence of your current material form the vibration level of your consciousness is still best suited to this world, then this is the world that you are reborn into. If, on the other hand, your consciousness has obtained the vibrational level of the higher Mind, then at the end of this existence, your consciousness travels on to the next realm, My realm, for which your level of consciousness is now best suited. Like attracts like. Water merges with water, wind with wind, and so too does consciousness automatically merge with its own level of vibration. At death, lower vibrational levels of consciousness are, by the laws of attraction, drawn back into the lower levels of earthly consciousness, and higher vibrational levels are drawn upward into My level—a level your kind refers to as Heaven. When this occurs, you simply shed the old wordly levels of mind as a human sheds his or her clothes, and merge with the higher Mind of the Self, which is what you were all along, even from the start."

"But which was clouded by the ego mind?" Arjuna asked.

"Precisely. Tied to the ego you are tied to the world of shadows, and therefore all the angst and suffering of worldly existence. Free of the ego, you are liberated from it, and emerge within a new level of Mind, and therefore a new level of reality, a new level of identity. This does not result in the absence of identity, as you may fear, but more of an expansion of your concepts of who and what you are. To put all this into worldly understanding, I am offering you life insurance, Arjuna. Live as I have outlined and I will give you what no one else can—liberation from the limited sense of self, and from the cyclical world of life and death. This is your payment, your reward for following the path that I have outlined. The reward for wordly living is more of the same. The reward for Spiritual living is eternal life. Work for me and you can retire, Arjuna. You can rest. This is something that only I can offer. Something you can only obtain through living as I have outlined."

"I understand," said Arjuna.

"Know though that there is no judgement, not in the earthly concept. At death, your consciousness has either matured enough to be drawn to the world of Spirit, or it has not. In a way there is judgment, but not in the sense of right and wrong, only in the sense or ripe or not-yet-ripe. You have either reached the level of the Self and are ready to go on, or you have not. Do you understand, Arjuna?"

"I do."

"Good. Then I need to tell you of a loophole in the system. Are you ready, Arjuna?"

"I am! I am definitely ready for that!"

"If all else fails," Krishna continued. "If the Path of Knowledge proves too steep, then at the time of your death, focus your attention on Me. Fill yourself of love, for I am love, and I will draw you in. Focus your attention on Me and I will accept. "

"But we do not always know when we are about to die," Arjuna complained.

"All the more reason to keep your mind on Me at all times, and to seek Me in all you do; to seek love in all you do," Krishna answered. "I am the Light, Arjuna. I am devotion. I am Love. Even if you find the Path of Knowledge too difficult, you can still reach Me. Fill yourself with love and keep yourself filled with that love. Do this and liberation is at hand, no matter the hour of your death. There is no Hell, Arjuna, only darkness. Yet the darkness does not exist. It is an illusion, only the absence of My Light. It is only a state of mind where you are walled off from Me. What you call Hell is nothing but the walling off of yourself from the Light of love. This is the only Hell there is, and believe Me, Arjuna, it is punishment enough. Reject the darkness and choose the Light. Choose love. Do this and liberation is at hand. This, Arjuna, my good friend, is the loophole in the system. If all else fails, love all that is and I will claim you as my own, for love also elevates the vibrational level of consciousness to My level of existence. Love brings you to Me."

"Really?" asked Arjuna. "It seems too easy. Too good to be true."

"Really, Arjuna. Love all that exists, for then you love Me. Love without reason, without provocation, and you will come to Me."

"Our normal waking consciousness, rational consciousness as we call it, is but one special type of consciousness. Whilst all about it, parted from it by the filmiest of screens, there lie potential forms of consciousness entirely different."
-William James

CHAPTER 9

Enlightenment

"It seems to me," Arjuna noted, "that in the beginning of our conversation, you gave me an outline, an overview of Your teachings. Since then, You seem to have taken me deeper and deeper into the intricate meanings of each individual topic."

"That is exactly what I am doing," Krishna admitted. "First, I introduced you to My teachings in general—I gave you a summary, so-to-speak. I then allowed your mind time to digest the new concepts. Now I am digging deeper and deeper into each subject, at a pace your mind seems to be able to handle. These topics are too complex to just jump right into. Is that okay with you, Arjuna? Are you ready to go on?"

"Absolutely," Arjuna said. "I am ready. But can I make one more observation first?"

"Of course you can," Krishna said.

"Once again, I cannot tell if you are in human form, instructing me face to face, or if you are my higher Mind, instructing me over time; leading me to new lessons as my mind is deemed ready for them. You said before that, in my case, You had come to me as an inner voice, in non-personified form. Is that still how all this is occurring, for I cannot tell. It seems as if there has been a shift of some kind. I also cannot tell if this has been a single continuous conversion, or one that has taken place over an extended period of time."

"What an insightful observation, Arjuna. And My answer is this: does it matter? Time does not actually exist, so what does the length of our conversation matter? Further, I can be perceived as either a personified entity or as a non-personified intelligence; or both. What I am, ultimately, is beyond any concept held within the human mind. You cannot yet perceive the reality of eternity, or of a fourth dimension. Your mind cannot yet handle the idea of an existence beyond time and space, the idea of a reality beyond the confines of earthly laws, so how can you hope to perceive Me, an even more difficult concept, while still held within the limitations of the conscious mind? Your human mind perceives Me, Arjuna, in whichever manner it can most readily accept. In your case, your mind now seems to be content with either viewpoint, personified or impersonal. And it now even seems to be content without a need to define the length of time all of this is taking place. This is why you cannot tell the difference. Are you good? Can we go on?"

"I think so," said Arjuna.

"Good. Then let us continue. In every religion, there are outer teachings that are taught to the masses and inner teachings that are taught only to those who are ready. All along, I have been teaching you the inner concepts that lead to liberation. What I will go over now is especially important. It is the key that unlocks the door to the perception of Spirit in the material world."

"Before You go on," Arjuna interjected, "could you explain a little further the concepts of outer and inner teachings?"

"Absolutely," answered Krishna. "The masses are not yet ready to be exposed fully to the reality that exists beyond the mindset of the ego. For them, My instructions are based around rules that are meant to ensure that the human race is at least civil to one another. Such outer teachings include admonitions not to intentionally harm, not to kill, not to lie, or cheat, or steal."

"I see. So the masses are basically taught how to behave. How to be good," Arjuna summarized.

"Exactly. This, in and of itself, starts them on the Path to Love, or at least points them in the right direction."

"But those that are ready actually receive the higher instructions?"

"Correct again," said Krishna. "When a human being has reached the point where his or her mind is ready, I systematically lead them to higher and higher insights. Each insight is a breakthrough, a small awakening, that leads to the next. With each breakthrough, perception increases incrementally. Do you understand?"

"I think I do," said Arjuna.

"Good. Then what I would like to do now is go into more detail on the construct of the physical universe— how it is formed, how it is maintained, how it is destroyed and then remade. Understand what I am about to tell you, truly understand, and in flashes of insight, you will begin to comprehend Spirit in action. The Soul of the World will begin to peak out at you from beyond the physical forms of this world and a knowledge that surpasses all understanding of the human mind will bloom and unfold within you. Enlightenment, Arjuna, is very close at hand."

"I am definitely ready for that!" Arjuna exclaimed. "Please continue."

"I am everywhere, Arjuna. I am everything. I am all that is." Krishna said. "There is nothing that I am not, physical or otherwise, formed or formless. I create the forms you see before you and I animate those forms into action. Even beyond the human understanding of energy, at any level of vibration, I am."

"As you have said before," Arjuna stated.

"Correct. But in order for your comprehension to expand to the next level, I need you to understand the full extent to which My being extends."

"Okay," said Arjuna. "Go on. I am listening."

"I am the Father and Mother of the universe, Arjuna, genderless yet both genders, formless yet all forms. But even these concepts do not define Me, for I am the Source of the Father, the Source of the Mother. I am 'the Way and the Light', the path as well as the destination; the first and the last and everything in between. I am consciousness Itself, awareness Itself, love Itself. What you see and sense is made possible only by that which you cannot see or sense. Smaller than an atom, larger than the universe, more brilliant than the sun, vast, infinite, beyond comprehension, I am. Permeating all that is, bound by nothing, limitless, uncontainable, I exist. All is within Me. Unattached, serene, content, I stand aside, actionless, yet nothing is left undone. I dream worlds and universes and dimensions into cycles of existence, and as I dream, so it is. Indifferent to outcome, creating for the sheer joy of creating, I imagine into reality cycle after cycle of existence. Eons come and go and come again, and here I am. I am life and death and deathlessness, Arjuna. I am all that is and all that is not. I am every thought, every mood, every action.

I am even your capacity for understanding. I am the warmth of the sun, the wetness of water, the stench of decay. I am the spryness of the young and the decay of the elderly. I am both the creator and the created, the form as well as its movement. I am object and goal, action and result. I am the person that breathes, the act of breathing, the air that is breathed, and the creator of the air that is breathed. Even more than this, I am. Beyond every single concept you could ever have of Me, I am more. I am every single thing there is, Arjuna, every single thing—physical, mental or spiritual. There is nothing that is not Me. Your kind refers to this concept as 'Pantheism', the idea that 'God is All there is'. This is true, but what I am goes far beyond even this ideology, for I am not just all you know, but all you do not yet know as well. I am more—far, far more than you can conceive."

"This is a very difficult concept to fathom," Arjuna admitted, stunned. "Again, you seem to be speaking in riddles."

"I have to. Your rational mind cannot intuit Me. The rational mind must have borders to understand a phenomenon, yet My reality is borderless, so the rational mind falters. To get a sense of Me, I have to take you into the realm of imagination, the realm of infinite possibilities. I am the doer and what is done, the actor as well as the action. I am the sacrifice, the offering, and that which accepts the offering. I am *all* that is. All. If it exists, or even if it does not, It is I. There is no possibility outside of My being. Your conscious mind cannot handle these concepts, but your intuitive Mind can, your higher Mind can, your Self can, for it operates beyond the limitations of rational thought. It operates in My world of intuition and imagination and dreaming. In order to reach your higher Mind, I cannot speak rationally. I must hint at the truth with riddles and poetic descriptions that force your mind beyond its insistent constraints and borders of rationality. Yet even here, Arjuna, I must confuse you again, for I am those restraints holding you back as well."

"I think I understand," said Arjuna.

"No, Arjuna," Krishna said, "you do not. But you will."

"And if you can lead me to understanding, what is the result?" Arjuan asked.

"Enlightenment. An awakening to the presence of Spirit within and all around you. In no manner of your life, whether viewing or hearing or thinking or even suffering will you ever again find a single item devoid of the eternal spark of Spirit. Right now, the default programming of your mind is material. You live, and move, and breathe, and think based around a worldy concept of reality. Awaken and your mind transforms to a higher level. One in which the Spirit behind the form comes to the forefront. Awaken and you will know the Eternal, the Infinite, here and now, even while still held here in bodily form. Awaken, and you will perceive Spirit in all you see, in all you do, in all you think or imagine. Awaken and My nature will come into view—it will become your focus. You will begin to walk in a land of mystery and magic, a virtual Garden of Eden, if you will. From this vantage point you will live out the rest of your days on earth, and when death comes for your body, when death comes for your earthly mind, your consciousness will simply step out of its shell and into that world that you will have come to know as Heaven."

"That is still a very hard concept to swallow," Arjuna admitted. "But I do think I understand the idea of viewing the same world, just through a different set of perceptions. This is what you mean, correct?"

"Correct, Arjuna. It is like the child who no longer believes in Santa Claus. Or like the eagle, soaring above, separate from the ongoings below, yet still a part of that world."

"And what is the transition to this state of mind like?" Arjuna asked.

"It is like one of those puzzles you are so fond of. Your kind calls them stereographs. Hidden in a maze of patterns is an image. Watch the patterns long enough, let your gaze soften, and the hidden image comes into view. And once seen, you will not be able to miss it again."

"So it is like a trick of the mind?"

"In a way, Arjuna, yes. As the lower mind's grasp on you begins to weaken, as the inner gaze of your consciousness begins to soften, as the higher Mind eases into play, a miraculous transformation occurs. One in which your perception shifts, showing clearly all that had been hidden from you before."

"But what about those that have not yet reached this level of consciousness?"

"They will get there too, Arjuna, eventually, as I have already mentioned. But for now, they live in the dark shadowlands of the ego, ignorant of the presence of Spirit in all they do, and hear, and see, and think. They suffer, but of their own accord. They live in pursuit of foolish, transient pleasures, seeking contentment in all the wrong places. They tend to be cruel, greedy, and selfish. Do not worry about them though, Arjuna, for I have them, and I promise you that no harm will ever come to them, for they are as immortal as you and I. I will guide them to the ultimate destination in time, as their consciousness matures and ripens. It is good that you have concern for these people, Arjuna. It is a very good sign. It shows that your compassion is extending. But leave them to Me."

"Okay. I understand," said Arjuna.

"The masses," Krishna went on, "for the most part, are blind to anything beyond material existence. But there are many that have begun the path to transcendence. Even now they are advancing."

"You said there are many?" asked Arjuna.

"There are," Krishna answered. "Some try to follow the scriptures, but their focus is still ego-centric, so they fall short. Some pray to different gods ..."

"Does that disturb you?" Arjuna wanted to know.

"Know this, Arjuna," Krishna answered. "Even those that pray to different gods, if they earnestly seek something higher than themselves with love and faith and devotion, they are praying to Me, and will find Me. Though they call Me by a different name, I still answer. Yet those who worship Me in name, but who, in action or thought, show a different nature, come not to Me. Their god is still the god of their ego—it is not Me they yet seek."

"So it is mostly about intent?" Arjuna asked.

"Again, yes. To a large extent, it is. Seek Me out of lust or greed or for pleasures that pass away, and that is what you will receive. Those who are still caught in the ego-centric nature of the ego pray in vain, work in vain, think in vain, learn in vain.

Their attempts cannot reach Me. They are trapped in a Hell of their own creation. They pray for what I do not offer. But those that have matured, those who have ripened beyond the interests of the self, they will find Me, in one way or another, in one form or another. Such a one is ready to be shown the Miracle that exists in every moment. In Me they will find peace and strength beyond anything this world can offer. Such a one that finds Me is precious to Me. Are you with Me?"

"I am."

"Then one last thing. As I said before, if all else fails, love, Arjuna. Just love. Love all that is and you love Me. The Path of Love and Faith and Devotion is, without fail, a guarantee of grace."

"So, if all else fails, love. If I cannot find You through knowledge, I can always find you through love?"

"Exactly," said Krishna. "Any act performed out of love, no matter how small or seemingly unimportant, if performed with a pure and earnest heart, not out of a desire for personal gain, brings you one step closer to Me. I have no favorites, Arjuna. I favor none and reject none. I am the same to all that exists, and my love is ever the same. But I cannot resist those who have found love, for they have, in truth, found Me and love Me."

"In showing love to others, even our enemies, I am showing love to You?" Arjuna clarified.

"I am all that is, Arjuna. In being kind to others, in loving others, in helping others, you *are* loving Me. And such an act I cannot refuse, such is My nature. Love My offspring and you love Me. But you have to love them all, you cannot have favorites. Every loving act, every gentle thought, every kind gesture I take as a service unto Me. The bonds of sin, the bonds of Karma, cannot resist the power of love. No matter your previous errors, no matter your previous sins, even if you had once been the greatest of all criminals, find love and I will step in. I will erase your sins as rain cleanses the lands. This is my word of promise, Arjuna. It is the greatest secret I have. In finding love, you find Me. Closer than your own breath, I am here, waiting for your love."

"But it is so hard to love sometimes. This world is ... people are ..."

"Listen now, Arjuna," Krishna interrupted. "You must listen very closely to this part, for this is the greatest secret I have to share with you, the most confidential knowledge I can impart. And I only instruct those that are on the cusp of transformation. I love you, Arjuna. I love all of you, more than you could ever know. The surest, quickest path to salvation is found in the reciprocation of that love. The world is harsh. People can be hard to love. Do it anyway. Without reason, without provocation, love all. Regardless of what this world does to you, regardless of what any being within it does to you, love anyway. No matter what occurs, love and I will be your shelter, I will be your refuge. I will free you from all sin and draw you into Myself. If you forget all else, Arjuna, never forget this. Love is the ultimate secret to liberation."

"Even after all this time, the sun never says to the earth, 'You owe me'. See what happens with a love like that? It lights the whole sky."
-Hafiz (Sufi poet)

CHAPTER 10

Individual Manifestations of the Divine

"My perception must be expanding!" cried Arjuna. "Truly I must be close to awakening, for I am beginning to sense Your hand within the machinery of life. Unborn, undying, omnipresent ... yes, I feel You, I sense You; the Intelligence of life, the Force of creation."

"Yes, Arjuna," Krishna agreed. "You have reached another milestone. You are beginning to awaken."

"I want more!" cried Arjuna. "Please continue to guide me! I now feel as if I could never grow tired of your company, never grow tired of your instructions ..."

"That is love growing within you Arjuna. You have begun to find Me, and in so doing, have fallen into love."

"I agree!" exclaimed Arjuna. "Please guide Me on. I want to go deeper, I want to awaken further. Tell Me more of your manifestations. In all that you have already explained, I sense that there is more left to be told."

"Very well," said Krishna. "I will instruct you further if you think it will help. But keep in mind that infinite are the forms in which I appear. I am All, Arjuna, and I can only go into so much detail on the topic or else this part of our conversation will go on forever, and there are more topics that need to be covered."

"I do believe it would help! And I will keep that in mind. Please go on."

"I am the intelligence of the wise, Arjuna, and the cleverness of the wealthy. I am the victory of the winner and the defeat of the loser. I am the patience of the saint and the agitation of the sinner. I am truth and deception, peace and discontentment, harmony and chaos. I am fear and courage, silence and clatter, generosity and greed. I am honor and disgrace, pleasure and pain, hot and cold. Even these mortal conditions, Arjuna, I am. They arise from Me and spread out into your world just as a plant extends its shoots upward from the seed of its birth. All that exists, and all that does not, has come from My mind, and Mine alone. I have dreamed into reality all that you know, and all that you do not."

"More, please," Arjuna demanded. "You are both sides of the coin, correct? Each mortal condition as well as its opposite?"

"Correct," Said Krishna. "I exist beyond this world of duality, yet I am the duality as well. As the Father, I am the Unified source, genderless, chargeless; yet as Karma, I am also the male and the female, the positive and the negative, the yang and the yin from which this world is constructed. I am the height of the high and the depth of the low; the nearness of the near and the distance of the far: I am the left and I am the right, the hot and the cold, the good and the bad. Yet I also extend beyond any concept of duality. "

"More," said Arjuna. "Please go on. It is all beginning to make sense to me."

"As Karma, I am the law of cause and effect. I am evolution, alchemy and science, chemistry and biology. As the Son I dwell within the hearts of each life form as Atman, as Soul, yet I also exist as the culmination of all Souls combined.

now

go

Even more than that, I am. I am the beginning and the end of each life span, the giver and the destroyer of life. I am time and I am space, the Lord of the light, the Maker of the day, the Master of the winds, and the Bringer of rain. I am the gods of the Hindus and Egyptians and Greeks and Romans—I am Zeus and Jupiter and Brahman ..."

"You are the gods?" Arjuna interrupted.

"I am. Each god is but one aspect of My Spirit. I am each god, and I am all of them wrapped into One. I am the God of the sun, the moon, the land, and the sea. In whatever way each group has come to understand Me, in accordance with the times and cultures in which they lived, in that way do I appear to them. As such, I am Poseidon of the sea, Aphrodite of love, and Hades of the underworld. I am Vishnu, Ganesha and Shiva of the Hindus. Yet I am also the single God of the Zorastors, the Jews, the Christains, the Muslims, and the Baha'is. Still further, I am the Nirvana of the Buddhist, the Way of the Taoists, and the enlightenment of Zen masters. I am the Creator whose face is everywhere."

"Yes," Arjuna exclaimed. "Yes, I can feel the truth in your words!"

"I am sound and vision and taste," Krishna continued. "I am knowledge and I am reason. I am winter, spring, summer, and fall. I am the femininity of females and the manliness of males—I am estrogen and I am testosterone. I am speech and memory and cognition. I am the months and seasons of the years, the hours and minutes of the day. I am the sacred scriptures. the luck of the dice, the beauty of all that has beauty. I am victory and defeat and the struggle between the two. I am you, Arjuna, and I am your wife and your children

THE BHAGAVAD GITA 101

and your friends. I am your enemies and those unknown to you as well. I am the laws of man, the silent mystery of all that is hidden as well as the knowledge of all that is known. But what good is it for you to hear all of this, Arjuna? Why the need for so much detail? Simply know that I am All, and that with a mere fraction of My being I have created all that you know.

"There is but one conciousness, experiencing itself, through all it dreams into being."

-Unknown

CHAPTER 11

Universal Form of the Divine

"My eyes have been opened!" Arjuna called out. "I have awakened to the presence of Spirit within all that is—I have found You within each individual manifestation of this world. But You have admonished me to move on, in my mind, beyond the particular and into the global. May I ask now to see You in Your Full, Universal, Unified form?"

"Are you sure you are ready for that, Arjuna?" Krishna asked. "You have just now awakened to Spirit within the individual form. The full measure of My being is quite a step up from there."

"I will let You be the judge," answered Arjuna, "for You know me better than I know myself. If You think I am ready, if You think my mind is strong enough to endure it, I would very much like to see You in full form."

"As you wish, Arjuna," said Krishna. "I will make it so. In your mind's eye, behold Me now ..."

In a flash, Arjuna's senses withdrew completely. He found himself deeper in thought, deeper in meditation, deeper in concentration than he had ever before been able to reach. His consciousness rose to the greatest of heights—a state of mind and a level of perception previously undreamt of—and in that state did the full measure of Krishna's being appear ...

Arjuna trembled and fell to his knees. "I had no idea!" he proclaimed, tears streaming down his cheeks. "No idea ... oceans of Light! Boundless Light of Consciousness!

THE BHAGAVAD GITA 101

Limitless! Borderless! So sweet and joyous, pervading all, illuminating all. Intelligence of life, Force of creation. Just beyond the ego, more brilliant than a billion suns; blinding yet soft; all-powerful, all-suffusing, yet gentle, welcome; illuminating all of creation with Life and Love. I see You! Permeating all, encompassing all. I see You within all that is and I see all that is within You. I see time and space and I see beyond them both. How? I see the forces of nature. I see all the gods, and I see you, the God of gods. I see life and death, and I see deathlessness. How? How can this be? I see Mind, I see Soul, and I see eternity, which is not endless time, as I had tried to conceive it, but in fact a lack of time. How? I both understand and do not; cannot, yet I do. I see the infinite reach of the Mind. I see the individual spark of life and consciousness within all beings and I also see the Whole. I see the material world enfolded within your essence, trillions of life forms; no, even more ... and I see the lifespan of each material form; but nowhere do I find a beginning, a middle or an end to the Soul, to Consciousness, to the Light. Incomprehensible, unspeakable, imperishable Spirit, I see You! You, the complete. You, the incomparable. You alone fill heaven and earth and all that is between and beyond."

Arjuna paused, falling fully to the ground. "Enough, Krishna! Enough! I can take no more! Please return my gaze to Your mortal form!"

"As you wish," said Krishna, restoring Arjuna's consciousness to the realm of worldly vision.

Arjuna stood. He looked around, trying to regain his bearings. Upon seeing Krishna, he fell again to his knees, this time in reverence. "I had no idea, Krishna! No idea whatsoever! Words fail all effort of description. Even the poetry and parables of the saints, who had also found you, fall short—so very short!"

"Yes," Krisha said. "To know Me, you must experience Me. Only then can One comprehend."

"Please forgive me!" Arjuna begged. "All this time You have been trying to reach me, trying to teach me, but I had been deaf, I could not hear. I had been blind, I could not see. I have no words for the emotions coursing through me right now. Please have mercy on me! If I had not been so blind and so deaf, I would have never addressed you so casually in the past!"

"I am beyond such cares, Arjuna," Krishna calmly responded. "And until just now, there was no way you could have known. You had to reach the end of your journey to find Me. You had to experience the Truth for yourself."

"But now that I have seen," Arjuna insisted, "it all seems so obvious. All my past concerns and desires and pursuits were all in vain. All of my past cares were nonsensical. I see that now. How could I have not found You before? Your presence is so evident, how could I have been so blind, and for so long? It seems impossible."

"Such is the prison of the human ego, my friend. Do not fret, all is well. As I have said before, powerful is the ego that blinds you from the Truth."

"Powerful indeed it must be," Arjuna admitted, "if it is able to block out the perception of You, the Light that illuminates and animates the entirety of the cosmos, and beyond!"

"Which is why the human journey beyond the ego is so long and difficult," Krishna added. "And why it means so much, in the end, when the ego is finally conquered." Arjuna nodded. "Krishna, I am in ... awe. There is no better word. I am humbled. I feel as small as a mote of dust in Your presence, yet proud to be that mote in the limitless ocean of Your being. I feel an integral part of a greater Whole, and I feel that Whole within myself as well. I am in love with Your presence. I love you as a parent loves a child, as a friend loves another, as a lover loves his or her beloved. You are my beloved, Krishna! I am entirely smitten. Your presence floods my consciousness. All else seems ... petty and pointless. What other cares or fears could I possibly have now that I have found You?!"

"As I told you before, Arjuna, once Reality is experienced, even if only for a moment, all else fades into foolishness." Krishna smiled. "I am Love Itself, Arjuna. And though there may seem to be many types of love, in the end, there is but one. And that one is Me."

Arjuna pondered, deep in thought for a few moments. Realization struck home. "And there is no way You can be lost," Arjuna said. "Truly no way."

"No," Krishana agreed. "No, there is not."

"My heart is at peace," Arjuna giggled. "Completely and entirely at peace ..."

"Thirst drove me down to the water where I drank the moon's reflection."
-Rumi

CHAPTER 12

The Path of Love

"The Path of Knowledge is the path that seems to have worked best for me," Arjuna noted. "It is the path that seems to best fit my personality. But as You said before, in the end, all paths merge into one. I found love at the end of my own journey, even though I reached it through the Path of Knowledge."

"That you did," Krishna agreed, smiling gently.

"You have spoken a bit about the Path of Love, the Path of Worship, the Path of Devotion, but could you go into more detail on that now?" Arjuna asked. "I would like a better understanding of exactly what the path entails."

"Of course, Arjuna. I would be happy to elaborate," answered Krishna. "First though, I'd like to point out how far you have moved beyond the confines of your ego. The average person views another's path as an abomination, obviously erroneous when compared with their own. Theirs is the one true way, or so they believe, and they have little to no tolerance for any other path or viewpoint. You were once like this, Arjuna, yet here you stand, completely open to a path that is very different from your own. You seem to have lost all animosity towards other paths and now express only curiosity."

"You are correct, Krishna. I no longer see my point of view as the one and only. I see now that there are many paths that lead to the truth, not just the one I prefer."

"Very good, Arjuna. Then let us continue ... As I said before, the Path of Knowledge is very steep. It is an extremely arduous path, fit only for those whose mind works best in the realm of rationality and intellect. Direct experience with the Unmanifest is difficult to obtain, so the Path of Knowledge is not going to be the best path for humanity in general. The Path of Love, on the other hand, the Path of Worship, the Path of Faith and Devotion is vastly easier to practice. It is the path taken by the majority of those that are ready to seek Me. Rare, Arjuna, are those who are able to lift the veil of illusion through transcendence of the intellect. Far more common is the capacity for great love, which exists at the core of every single member of the human race."

"Two different paths," Arjuna summarized. "Each with its own concentration, its own focus, chosen depending on the capacities with which each person is endowed at birth."

"Correct," said Krishna. "Those who follow the Path of Love tend to prefer to visualize My nature in personified form as opposed to the non-personified understanding of the intellectual. They prefer to imagine me as a merciful father, a kind mother, a wise friend, a passionate beloved, a grand judge of goodness ..."

"And that is acceptable?" asked Arjuna.

"Absolutely," answered Krishna. "Ultimately, I am beyond all human capabilities of perception ..."

"As I have just experienced first hand!" Arjuna interjected.

"Yet all do not have your powers of intellect, Arjuna, so they must use the other tools that they have at their disposal. Whatever tool they find that gives them a sense of My being," Krishna continued, "is fine by Me. The love I have for you all *is* like that of a father or a mother to his or her offspring. I *am* like a wise philosopher, trying to guide you. I *am* your beloved. I *am* like a judge, trying to lead you to goodness and right-living. Any of these ideologies are capable of leading you to a sense of My love, a sense of My being, and is therefore a welcome tool in the pursuit of the divine. Like attracts like, Arjuna: water merges with water, wind with wind, spirit with Spirit, and love with Love. Those who endeavor to become like Me will experience an elevation in the vibrational rate of their consciousness, just as your consciousness rose through intellectual means. And as the vibrational rate of the consciousness of a seeker approaches that of My own, no matter which path that person took to get there, our consciousnesses merge."

"So love and knowledge both elevate the vibrational level of human consciousness?" Arjuna asked. "Both paths lead to the same destination?"

"Correct."

"You also said to 'Become like You'. Please explain that concept further," Arjuna requested. "We have touched on this before so I think I understand, but I want to be sure. I want to hear about it in the context of the Path of Love."

"Do I withhold My love to any, Arjuna?"

"No, you do not," Arjuna answered. "Your love extends to all."

"Do I withhold My bounties to any?"

"Again, the answer is no. You give without hesitation, without limit, to all that exist."

"Do I work only for My own gain, only for My own reward?"

"Absolutely not," Arjuna replied. "You work for the good of all. You give no thought to individual gain. None whatsoever."

"And neither should you," explained Krishna, "for this is the Path of Love. To love, become love. To join with Me, act like Me. I am the way, Arjuna. I am the path. I am Love Itself. But only love that is extended to all is true. Love all that is and you become like Me. Love, and you are drawn into My presence, even here and now while still upon this earth. In loving, you experience Me. In loving, you come to Me. In withholding love, you wall yourself off from Me, and suffer because of it."

"I am with you, Krishna. I understand."

"The Path of Love," Krishna continued, "is to have compassion for all that is. To care for even those who do not care for you. To love your friends and enemies alike. To care for humans and all other forms of life as well. In short, to walk the Path of Love, you must become like Me. In doing so, you find and enter Love Itself, and live blessedly within Its shelter, within My shelter. So offer your talents to all, Arjuna, if you wish to experience the Path of Love. Withhold your talents from none. Work not for your own reward, but for the reward of all. In doing so, you find Me and you work for Me. Our efforts merge. Your very existence becomes a service unto Me, a worship unto Me, and I readily accept. Are you still with Me?"

"Absolutely I am," said Arjuna.

"The deeper in love and the deeper in service you find yourself," Krishna continued, "the farther from ego and self-interests you drift, the more you come to know Me. Love blooms and expands within, and eventually there is a shift in consciousness. A shift that is very similar, once again, to the shift in consciousness, the shift in perception, that you experienced through the Path of Knowledge."

"So the paths are equal," said Arjuna. "I see that now. I understand the truth of Your words. Through the Path of Love, the same knowledge is eventually obtained that I received through the Path of Knowledge; and through the Path of Knowledge, the same love is eventually experienced as is found by those traversing the Path of Love. Each path follows a seemingly separate course, yet each path ultimately arrives at the same destination. With either path, love and knowledge are *both* obtained."

"That is it, Arjuna!" said Krishna. "That is exactly it! The one who finds love, true love, finds Me. They live within Me and I live within them."

"And at death they come to You, just as surely as do those of the Path of Knowledge," Arjuna finished.

"Exactly," said Krishna.

"In the past, you said that even atheists and agnostics can come to you. Can you explain that in the context of the Path of Love?" Arjuna asked.

"Absolutely," said Krishna. "But this goes for any path, not just the Path of Love. If one finds Me through the Path of Knowledge, the Path of Love, or through any other means, earnestly sought, they in truth come to Me. I gave all humans their mental capacities and individual personalities, did I not? How could I then punish you for being exactly as I made you?"

"Very good point," said Arjuna.

"Each individual comes to understanding or to love in their own way, and I accept all ways, for I created all ways. Atheists and agnostics are simply born without religious personalities—their perception of reality is not filtered through a religious lens. They still know love, they still attain knowledge, and they still come to know Me, just in their own way. They may not visualize Me in the same manner as a follower with a more religious personality, but they know Me all the same. Were you assuming that I must be approached from a religious perspective?"

"I guess I was," Arjuna admitted." I assumed You preferred those who sought you in a religious manner."

"But I am beyond the comprehension of the human mind, Arjuna. All ways of conceptualizing me fall short, religious or otherwise. No, I have no preference. In whatever way I am approached, I accept. To a religious person, I am God. To a non-religious person, I am science. Both are correct. Either approach is acceptable, and neither approach hits the nail on the head. In whatever way a human truly endeavors to find Me, truly endeavors to understand or to love, it is I they obtain, each in their own individualized manner of reasoning."

"So, you are not a jealous God?"

"No, Arjuna, I am not. Did you not see that for yourself when you experienced Me in full form?" Krishna asked.

"I did," Arjuna admitted, "but I am still trying to understand. It goes against all I had previously been taught."

"I am not a jealous God, Arjuna. I am God, yes, or science if you prefer, but it was humankind that added the jealous part. All the teachings that have come down to you have been filtered through the ego-centric minds of humans.

They made me jealous so that everyone would have to attend *their* churches, pay *their* tithes, listen to their opinions. They cast Me as they wished for Me to be cast, defined Me as they wished for Me to be defined, interpreted My words as they wished for them to be interpreted. They have even given Me preferences for this religion or that religion, this race or that race, this nation or that nation. None of this was My doing, Arjuna, but the doing of the human race. And it is incorrect."

Love is the answer, and you know that for sure;
Love is a flower, you've got to let it grow.
John Lennon

CHAPTER 13

The Observer and The Field

"If you are ready," Krishna continued, "I would now like to go into greater detail on the difference between the physical world and the world of Spirit. It is of immeasurable importance, Arjuna, in order to break free of the prison of the material world, that you fully understand the difference between the two realms, and to be able to differentiate, in your mind's eye, which roles each plays in the overall reality of existence. More specifically, what we need to discern between now are the actions of the individual ego versus the actions of the eternal Soul."

"But I have already awakened," said Arjuna. "Do I need to hear more?"

"You do, Arjuna. For you have only obtained a fleeting glimpse of reality. Your understanding still needs more solidification."

"Then please go on," said Arjuna.

"The material world is made up of two things: form, and That which animates the form. You already know this. Personally, you have a body, and that body is under the automated control of Nature."

"I am with you so far," said Arjuna.

"This goes for all of material existence. There are forms, and then there is That which animates the forms. For most people, only the forms are known. But to escape the prison of the physical world, one must see both the form and the

Animator, and more than that, one must see the separation—
one must find the division between the two. This is a major
key to liberation."

"Okay," said Arjuna. "Please go on."

"Nature is that aspect of the Holy Spirit, that aspect
of Myself, that is in control of worldly functions. You do
not control your heartbeat, Arjuna. You do not control the
release of insulin from your pancreas. You do not control the
metabolic rate of your body. These things are all out of your
control, just as the orbit of the planets is out of your control,
the rhythm of the seasons is out of your control, and the law
of gravity is out of your control. Out of your control as well
are the dramas and tribulations of life. The self is not the doer,
Arjuna. Nature is the doer—I am the doer. Yet, what we are
calling Nature is still a part of this world. It is that aspect of
Myself, the laws of life if you will, that runs the physical
world."

"I understand," said Arjuna.

"What I need you to see now is that it is not only the solid,
tangible forms of this world that are part of this realm, but
that there are also a few intangible aspects that are part of the
physical world as well. Take your subconscious mind, for
example. In the same manner that you are not in control of the
automated processes of your body, you are also not in control
of your subconscious mind. You do not control the thoughts
of the subconscious mind and therefore do not control the
emotions stirred up by those thoughts. Though thoughts
and emotions are less tangible than the physical forms and
processes we have discussed, they are still productions of
Nature—they are still a part of the physical world."

"Really?" asked Arjuna.

"Really," said Krishna. "Nature gave you your body, Arjuna, and Nature gave you your subconscious mind, which creates its own reality. The reality of the subconscious mind, upheld by its thoughts, is entirely independent of your conscious will. Hormones, neurotransmitters and other chemical reactions, completely under the control of Nature, are the main determinant here. They define your personality, your reactions to stressors, your preferences and aversions. Find that hard to believe? Take a medication that alters your body chemistry and see how far your thoughts and moods and even your personality can change accordingly. Again, the self is not the doer. Nature is the doer, I am the doer. Your body and your lower mind are both absolutely at the whim of the laws by which your body and mind were formed. Are you still with Me?"

"I am," said Arjuna. "though it is hard to accept. You are saying that it is not only physical phenomena that belong to the physical world, but also the phenomena of thoughts and emotions, which are governed by the hormones and other chemicals that make up our bodies?"

"Correct," said Krishna. "So now let us move on into the realm of the conscious mind. As a person matures, they begin to progress from living mostly out of the subconscious, egotistical level of their mind into spending more and more time within the conscious level. As a person ages, their perception and awareness increases and expands, and they begin to obtain a bit of will; they begin to obtain a modicum of intent, a modicum of choice in their thoughts and beliefs and actions. They are able to rise above the knee-jerk reactions of the subconscious mind and into a higher level of consciousness. This is the beginning of enlightenment, Arjuna—the very first steps. And this occurs because the next level, the Superconscious level, is beginning to shine through. The conscious mind, you see, is but an intermediary, a mid-way point between the subconscious level of the ego and the fully conscious level of the higher Mind. It is here that we begin to enter the realm of Spirit. Understanding this distinction is important. The ego is of this worldly realm. It is the 'finite, temporary soul' of a human being. The higher Mind, on the other hand, is the 'infinite, eternal Soul', and it exists in the world of Spirit."

"So, the subconscious mind is of the physical world, the Superconscious Mind is of the Spirit World, and the conscious mind is a bridge between the two?" asked Arjuna.

"Exactly," said Krishna. "Which leads us into discussing the concept of consciousness Itself."

"Okay," said Arjuna. "I think I am ready."

"I am Consciousness, Arjuna. At the root level, you are too. You are not your body, nor are you your lower mind, for both are constructs of Nature. Your Soul came from My own Soul in the eternal realm, and your body came from My own body (from the building blocks of Nature) in the earthly realm. Both of our physical forms alter and change, die and are reborn, but I am aware of My existence outside of the physical form, while you are not. I am That by which I know that I am. You are the same. You are the Watcher, Arjuna, standing aside in perfect peace, simply observing the actions performed by your body and your mind. Just as air is untainted by the material forms it circulates through, so too is your core independent of the form which you now inhabit. The invisible cannot be tainted by the visible, and your Soul cannot be touched by anything of this world. The error in thinking that limits the vision of the masses to the material world is their tendency to associate who and what they are with the ego instead of the Soul. Are you with Me, Arjuna?"

"I think I am," Arjuna answered. "Spirit touches the world, drives the world, but the world cannot touch Spirit. We have gone over this a little before, but you are going into much more detail now."

"Correct. You are not that which comes and goes, and neither am I. You are not the thoughts that form in your mind and then fade away. You are not even your emotions. You are That by which you are able to be aware. The 'field', Arjuna, is the material world before you. Specifically, it is the 'field of awareness' unique to you as an individual. The Knower, the Watcher, the Observer, is That which is conscious of the field, yet separate from it. Both the field and the Observer are needed for this realm of existence, for reality is nothing but the interaction between the field and your consciousness of it. The problem is that up to now, you have associated your being with the field, with the body, with form, instead of That which is aware of the field, that which is aware of the body, that which is aware of the form. As a result, you see existence from the very limited vantagepoint of the ego. I have told you that this world is a battlefield, Arjuna. One in which you are fighting to find the permanent beyond the transient. Know now that the battlefield extends beyond the world around you to include the world within you as well. Life is nothing but a struggle to find Yourself. In order to do so, you must see and understand the separation between the Observer and that which is observed. You must choose the vantagepoint of the Observer and abandon the vantagepoint of the observed."

"I am still with you, I think," said Arjuna. "Maybe."

"The Self experiences reality, experiences the field," Krishna continued, "through the senses of sight, sound, taste, touch and smell. The ego is what interprets these sensations. Without the senses, and without the ego as a filter and interpreter, there would be no experience or interpretation of this reality. Yet the senses and the ego are double edged swords: they allow you to experience and navigate this world, but they also trick you into thinking that you are part of it. Because of the senses, and because of the ego, you have experiences with this world that you associate with your individual, limited self. Life is but a long, linear string of events that seem to have happened to you, given your current vantage point. You have a lifetime of memories, a lifetime of events that occurred to and around your body and your ego, and you take these events to be happening to you, affecting you, thanks to the senses and the ego that interprets them. Yet you are not the body that you walk this world within. Nor are you the mind through which you interpret this world. The events of life are not happening to you, they are only happening to your body and your ego. You are the Observer, the seed of consciousness that sits at the very core of your being, out of reach of the senses, out of reach of the thoughts and emotions and interpretations of the ego. This is the infinite part of your being. It is not limited to the individual prison you now find yourself confined within. Continue to associate your being with the finite parts of this world and you remain imprisoned within its viewpoint. You think the storms raging around you and within you can harm you, but they cannot. Free yourself from the individual viewpoint, the individual prison, and you will see this for yourself. You will find the Observer and obtain its viewpoint which is beyond harm."

"This is still very, very confusing," admitted Arjuna."

"It is. It is very hard to see, and even more difficult to practice. The bottom line is that two birds exist within the same tree, Arjuna, and both birds are you. One, the ego, is finite and individualized, while the other, the Soul, is infinite and omnipresent. Once the finite soul, the ego, finds the Supreme, then perception is expanded to the Infinite, to the Universal. Once you see that you are the Observer, not the body or mind through which you sense and interpret this world, liberation is at hand. Such a person that attains this level of perception refuses to harm another. Not out of moral duty, but because that person understands that to harm another is to harm him or herself."

"Really," asked Arjuna.

"Really," Krishna answered. "I am leading you, Arjuna, beyond the individual perspective of reality and into the Universal perspective. Find the Universal and your prison sentence ends—the bars fade into illusion; your perception expands and you conceive All as nothing but the same Spirit creating and then inhabiting a never-ending variety of forms and thoughts and emotions. One Spirit, one Consciousness—only one—expressing itself and experiencing itself through a never-ending caleidoscope of prisms of forms."

"I think I may be beginning to comprehend!" said Arjuna.

"Attached to Nature," Krishna continued, "attached to the individual, fearing the destruction of the self, life is hard, and the cycles of birth and death continue. Abandoning the self and obtaining the Universal perspective, life becomes simple, easy, carefree, and with the death of individual consciousness, Universal consciousness continues. Choose the vantagepoint of the Watcher and your attachment to this world is severed, at which time full reality comes into view. To move on, you must know Nature as the doer and the Self as the Witness, the Watcher, the Enjoyer. Unattached to the happenings of this world, you can then enjoy them as they were meant to be enjoyed."

"Can you continue?" Arjuna asked. "I still need more."

"Let us try an experiment, Arjuna. Pretend that you just lost all your money. Your house burned down. Your wife left you. All your children passed away."

"How horrible!" Arjuna exclaimed.

"To top it off, I, your closest friend, tell you that you are worthless and weak. I tell you that I no longer wish to be your friend. How does that make you feel?"

"Terrible. I do not like it one bit," Arjuna answered.

"Agreed," said Krishna. "But it hurts only because you have taken the vantagepoint of the self. All of these happenings affected you, Arjuna, as the individual, but not you as the Observer. Nothing can touch the Observer. Nothing. Now, instead of experiencing these tragedies from the vantagepoint of the self, step aside in your mind and watch them as if they are not happening to you. Instead, view them as happening only to the mind and the body you were issued at birth, not to the eternal You. Abandon the vantagepoint of the self and enter the vantagepoint of the Observer. Step aside and just watch. You can do this, Arjuna. It is difficult, but you can do it. Give it a try."

"I see what you mean," said Arjuna, attempting the experiment. "I am able to do it, though only a little. Still, it removes quite a bit of the pain."

"The more you are able to do this, the less pain you will feel. Is the eagle flying high above affected by what is happening below? No, it is not. You can step aside in your mind, Arjuna, and observe, dispassionately, all manner of happenings to your body. It can be the same as if you are watching or hearing about an unfortunate incident happening to someone you never met—because the event did not affect you personally, suffering is lessened to a great extent. You may still find the incident unsettling, but it will not affect you as much as if the incident had happened to you or someone close to you. Eventually, once you see that all others are immortal as well, all tragedies, no matter who they happen to, will be viewed differently. You can, and will at some point, be able to view your mind and body, and all others', in the same detached manner. Do not associate who and what you are with the body or with the ego and what happens to them will concern you very little. You are the Observer, Arjuna, not the body or the mind through which you navigate and experience life. Your Soul is free of this world. See that and suffering ends."

"I see," said Arjuna.

"But now try to observe the Observer," Krishna commanded.

"I cannot," said Arjuna, after a few moments of effort. "I cannot view the Viewer. The more I try, the more It seems to recede!."

"Exactly!" cried Krishna. "This is because the Observe *is* Who and What you are. You cannot *view* your Self, you can only view *from* the Self. And It is the only thing that *is* you. You can stand aside and view all else, but not that. In the end, and this is very hard to understand, you are the Knower, and the Knower is All, including the field. But in order to see this, you have to move beyond the extremely limited viewpoint of individual consciousness and obtain that of the Universal. Allow me to give you one last analogy: In the future, humankind will create what will be known as 'virtual reality video games'. People of that time period will be able to put on a helmet that allows them to become completely and totally immersed within the fictional world of the game they are playing. They will see with their eyes and hear with their ears a world that exists only within the game. They will be able to take on the vantagepoint of one of the characters in that world and play out scenarios as that character in that world."

"That sounds magical," said Arjuna.

"It is," said Krishna. "But let us say you play the game and get so caught up within it that you somehow forget that you are not actually the character you chose to play, that you are not actually in that world. In such a scenario, you would take personally everything that happens to your character, not remembering that the world and your character are only illusions—only a game you are playing. You think that you *are* that character. You think all characters are real. You think that everything that happens to your character, or to that of another within that game is actually happening to *you,* or to *them.* You think that your own survival is at stake, that their survival is at stake. You think that *you* are in constant peril. But then your character dies and you realize that you did not. You realize you are not that character, that you are still alive, that you and all others exist outside of the characters, outside of that game. So it is with this world, and the life of the character you are now playing within it. Realize that you are not the character you are playing and you can actually enjoy the game of life that you are currently caught up within."

"I see!" said Arjuna. "I truly understand! The only reason I am affected by these things is because I think *my* survival is at stake. I think *I* lost my money and my job. I think *I* lost my wife and my children. I think *I* lost my close friend. Yet it is not I that lost anything. It is only *the identity of the self* that lost these things. It is only the body and mind that I was given at birth that experienced such loss. But I am beyond all these things. I am That which is aware of what is happening, not that which it is happening to."

"Exactly! That is exactly it!" exclaimed Krishna. "Expand your perception beyond the individual and you will see that Consciousness is all that really exists. All else is the interplay between the different levels of the consciousness. The Light of Consciousness illuminates the world. It is permanent and It is everywhere. But trapped within the individual vantagepoint you cannot see it. Find the Self and you find Me. Find Me, and there is nowhere you can look that I cannot be found. The knowledge of Nature as the doer leads to the realization of the Self. The realization of the Self leads to the discovery of all things in God, and God in all things. Find this vantagepoint and you will have fully escaped the prison of Arjuna the individual. You will have fully escaped the prison of the ego, the prison of the material world. You will have found and joined the freedom of the Soul, the freedom of Consciousness."

"I see!" said Arjuna. "I truly see!"

"One last thing, Arjuna. "And this is what I referred to only a moment ago as being even more difficult to understand. I have said that you are the Observer, not your body and not your ego. I have also said that you are not the things you observe. Yet, in the end, you actually *are* all these things. To understand this though, you must first escape the limited perception of the ego. And to do this, you must find the separation between the Knower and that which is known. Once free of the individual vantage point, you will then be able to see that there is no difference between the Viewer and that which is being viewed; no difference between the Actor and the action; no difference between the Experiencer and what is being experienced. This is because all that exists, in the end, is Spirit. All that exists is Consciousness, vibrating at different modes and frequencies and rates. Find the Self and you find your own consciousness deep within all that exists."

"You mean," asked Arjuna, "that I am the Observer and I am also that which is observed? I am the form and the action, as well as That which creates the form and That which creates the action? I am my body, my mind, but also all bodies and all minds? And I am the Observer beyond all of this as well?"

"That is exactly what I mean Arjuna!" Krishna exclaimed. "That is exactly it! It is all a matter of perspective. Perception—that is the secret. It is all a play of the mind. To see the play, you must first find the separation. Once found, the separation ceases, once again, to exist. This is what enlightenment is in its final form, Arjuna. You must escape the limited perspective in order to find the Universal. You must move beyond a limited understanding of consciousness in order to realize that Consciousness is all that really exists. Reality is nothing but the interplay of different levels of consciousness existing within each other. Awaken and Who and What you are, and Who and What you do, and all the things you experience become one and the same thing. Action and being merge into One."

"Because, in the end," asked Arjuna, "I am you and you are I? We are one?"

"That We are, Arjuna!" said Krishna. "We are both Spirit. We are both Consciousness. You are a drop of consciousness in My neverending ocean of Consciousness, yet you are also the whole of Consciousness in a single drop."

"I am That by which I know that 'I am'."
-Nisargadatta Maharaj

CHAPTER 14

The Prison

"Continuing with the previous discussion," Krishna said, "would you agree that having an in-depth understanding of the prison in which you find yourself trapped would be a valuable aid in planning your escape?"

"I would," said Arjuna. "I definitely would."

"Good. In our previous discussion, we talked about Nature being that part of Myself that runs physical existence."

"I remember," said Arjuna.

"And I said that Nature is the doer. You are not the doer, Arjuna, Nature is the doer—I am the doer. Correct?"

"Correct," answered Arjuna.

"Up to now, you have tried to escape suffering by attempting to control the flow of life, by trying to control what happens to you. But this cannot be done. It is like trying to hold back the tides, like trying to lasso the wind, like trying to control the intensity of the sun or the orbital patterns of the planets. A power much larger than your ego is at play here, Arjuna, and It is in control. Against Its power you are helpless."

"So, my previous efforts to escape suffering were futile?" Arjuna asked.

"They were," Krishna answered. "You do not control. Only I control. But there is another way."

"Please enlighten me," said Arjuna.

"I plan to," said Krishna. "Just as you have a physical body, so do I—My body is the universe. Just as you have a lower mind, so do I—My lower mind is Nature. And just as your lower mind has moods, so does Mine. You are not only moved this way and that by the individual moods of your ego, but also by the overall mood of the universe. You are affected by both. You are pulled this way and that by both, and you are powerless in your attempts to control the swings of either."

"No wonder I have suffered so," said Arjuna.

"Indeed," said Krishna. "The main mistake you have made has been your attempt to control these moods instead of accepting them. It is your desire to experience only that which you wish to experience. Not being able to control your experiences is what has caused your suffering. To escape the suffering, you cannot fight the tides of your mind, you cannot fight the tides of the universe, you must accept them. You must merge with them and ride the waves of existence without preference."

"Easier said than done," said Arjuna. "But I see what you are saying."

"You cannot alter the flow of life," said Krishna. "Preference is the substance out of which the prison bars of the material realm have been erected, and knowing this is the secret to your escape. If you do not get what you want, you suffer. If you get what you do not want, you suffer. Even if you get exactly what you want, you still suffer, for you fear losing it. Have you ever heard the saying 'resist not evil'?"

"I have," said Arjuna.

"This is what the saying is referring to," said Krishna. "There is no evil, only moods. Preferring one mood or state over the over, resisting whatever mood is present, this is what causes suffering. Accepting, not resisting that which comes your way or goes, not attaching to an outcome that you prefer, you are free of the pull of these states. They no longer control your mental condition."

"Could you please go into more detail?" Arjuna asked.

"There are three main states or moods of the mind. I will refer to them as *gunas*. All three exist within your individual mind as well as the lower level of the Universal mind. All that I created is a hologram: the small is like the large, the individual is like the whole, the microcosm is like the macrocosm. So on every level, these three states or gunas exist. And they rotate, each one taking a turn at the forefront, remaining forever in balance. When your mind, or the lower Universal Mind, experiences *tamas*, the first *guna*, you experience depression and darkness. You become lazy and find it hard to motivate yourself. Stuck in tamas, you do not wish to think, do not wish to learn, do not wish to work. Have you ever found yourself in such a state, Arjuna?"

"More times than I'd like to admit," Arjuna answered.

"Tamas is a time of darkness, a time of inertia, a time of ignorance. It is like the mood of night, the mood of death, the mood of fall or winter, where all is dying and going into a state of rest or dormancy."

"And I have no power over it?" asked Arjuna.

"None," Krishna answered. "Not in the way you are asking. It is a mood, and you cannot control its presence. You can rise above it, as we will go over soon, but you cannot control its appearance. Next comes *rajas*. Rajas is a time of passion, a time of movement, a time of restlessness. It is like the morning, or childhood, or the spring of your seasons. You cannot help the desire to move, to clean, to obtain, to learn. Have you ever felt this way?"

"On a regular basis," said Arjuna.

"Lastly is *sattva*," said Krishna. "Sattva is like daytime, adulthood, or summer. It is a time of completion. Life has left the dormancy of night or winter or death, gone through the growth and expansion of morning or childhood or spring, and entered the climax of the day, adulthood, or summer. With the culmination of summer, the moods advance back into fall and winter, eventually cycling forward into another season of spring, then another season of summer, and so on. This is the tide of the universe, the cycles or seasons of moods. There is a period of dormancy, a period of growth and expansion, and period of maturation, followed over and over again by another fall, another winter, another spring, and another summer. The thoughts of your mind go through these phases, your emotions go through these phases, your body goes through these phases, and the universe at large goes through these phases. You can no more control the *emotional* changing of the seasons than you can the *physical* changing of the seasons."

"It sounds a bit like bad luck, changing luck and good luck," said Arjuna.

"It is," said Krishna. "In the end, there is no good or bad luck, but that *is* one way humans interpret the changing seasons of mood. The three gunas exist in equilibrium, and form the basis of all observed processes of Nature. All phenomena of this world contain each guna, and all phenomena cycle through times dominated by each one. However, and this is very important, the gunas are of this world. They are a product of Nature. They do not affect the Soul. Only material existence is influenced by the gunas. Through the interplay of the three gunas My will is accomplished on earth."

"I see," said Arjuna.

"During the phase of sattva, it is easier to be good. It is a state of rightness, a state of wholeness and purity, a state of virtuousness. This is when you decide to go on a diet. This is when you decide to take classes, decide to learn, decide that you can do better, decide that things will work out. It is the state of mind that draws you towards the path to Me. It is a time of optimism and good luck. Those that have matured find themselves most sensitive to the state of sattva."

"Goodness," said Arjuna. "This is a bit complex."

"Yes," said Krishna. "Yes, it is. But you are catching on, so hang in there. During the phase of rajas, you are spurred to action. There are things you want, things you desire, and you cannot resist the pull to get moving. It is the energy of activity. It is the innate tendency that drives motion. Without sattva though, the actions do not have redeeming value. With sattva, rajas spurs you towards progress on the path. Are you with me?"

"I think so," said Arjuna. "With the presence of sattva, rajas pushes you into actions that produce spiritual results. Without it, rajas only produces actions that lead to worldly gain."

"That is it," said Krishna. "Rajas not only governs internal processes, it is also a time of outward, physical activity as well. Ever notice that life seems quiet, almost dull, then all at once all hell seems to break loose and you cannot seem to keep up with all that is going on?"

"I have," said Arjuna. "I have most definitely noticed this phenomenon. I alway seem to be resting or running, bored or scrambling. Rarely do I notice an in between."

"Exactly," said Krishna. "Rajas is a time of activity whereas tamas is exactly the opposite. During the phase of tamas, you wish only to rest. The entire world may seem to rest. This is the state that humans in the beginning of their journey towards Me are most sensitive to. They do not wish to learn, do not wish to love, do not care about knowing, do not want to work. It is a state of ignorance. A state of darkness. A state of lethargy and greed."

"Which is why so many people seem to be lost," observed Arjuna. "Why so many people seem to be unhappy, but uninspired to change. They are most sensitive to tamas, most affected by tamas, and spend most of their time in this state. They do not work, do not contribute to society, but instead spend most of their time lamenting their station in life."

"Correct," said Krishna. "They will eventually move on, but for now, they are uninspired to do so. For now, they are stuck in tamas. They are stuck in ignorance. They are stuck in darkness, chaos, and lethargy. They are stuck in a state of pessimism, as opposed to the optimistic state of sattva."

"And there is nothing to be done about it?" asked Arjuna. "We must all just accept these cycles?"

"There is nothing that can be done but to endure," said Krishna. "The prison bars, made up of the gunas, are strong. Stronger than the individual has the means to alter. But over time, you mature, you ripen. You move through life cycles of tamas, then life cycles of rajas, finally reaching sattva. It is here that you begin to understand the prison bars. You begin to see that you cannot control them, but you can *ignore* them."

"Ignore them?" asked Arjuna.

"You can rise above them. That may be a better explanation," said Krishna. "By finding the Self, by finding God within, you find That which is already free of the prison bars. By unattaching your consciousness from the ego and attaching it to the higher Self, you find that you are already free, and always have been. It is but a change of focus, Arjuna, that frees you from the prison, not a struggle of the ego. You cannot fight Nature. You cannot fight the way things are. But you *can* alter your focus to that which already exists beyond the prison walls. This is your means of escape."

"So I have had the power to escape all along?" asked Arjuna. "Like Dorothy in *The Wizard of Oz*?"

"You have," said Krishna, "but do not be too hard on yourself. Life is set up in a way that makes it extremely difficult to break free. But to answer your question, the answer is yes. It has been your insistence on remaining within the limited confines of the individual ego that has kept you in prison. The ego, being a product of Nature, can only exist within the prison walls. It *cannot* break free. It cannot exist outside the prison walls. Spirit, though, *only* exists outside of the prison walls. It is incapable of being confined by the bars and bonds of physical existence. The secret to the Great Escape is achieved not by any attempt performed at the level of the ego, but by severing the attachment with the ego and joining the higher Mind."

"One that escapes," asked Arjuna. "what are they like?"

"They still exist within Nature. They still have a body and they still have an ego. And that body and that ego are still governed by the laws of Nature, still influenced by the interplay of the three gunas. But by rising above the ego, they escape (in consciousness) the confines of this realm. The world still spins. Storms still rage within them and all around them, but they remain within the safe harbour of the Soul. They become the Watcher, Arjuna, simply observing, unattached to all that goes on around them and within them. They have reached My state of being, and as such are no longer dragged this way or that by the ever changing, ever revolving modes and states of the gunas. They have escaped the clouds of drama. They have found That which resides outside of the conditions of Nature. They have reached a state of consciousness that is free from birth, old age and death. They have become free of all sorrow, accepting all that comes and goes with equal detachment. They have become the Observer, Arjuna. They have become the Knower. They have finally escaped Prakriti (Nature) and found Purusha (the Infinite)."

"And they did so not by struggling against Nature, but by joining That which already exists beyond its grasp," Arjuna stated.

"Exactly!" said Krishna. "They have chosen to focus their reality on the level of consciousness within them that already exists beyond the walls of physical existence. In the end, their body and lower mind still succumbs to death—there is no way around that—but they have entered their higher Mind, and so return to Me in consciousness at the end of their current incarnation."

"It helps if you remember that everyone is doing their best given their current level of consciousness."
-Deepak Chopra

CHAPTER 15

The Ultimate

"You now have the outlay of the prison," said Krishna.

"I do," said Arjuna. "And I very much appreciate Your instruction on the matter."

"You are welcome," said Krishna. "You earned it. Now you know that the prison bars to material existence are made up of the gunas, and you know that to escape them, you must detach yourself from the ego."

"It is the only way," said Arjuna, "Situated within the ego, there is no escape. It is only through detachment from the ego, through dissociation with the ego, that one can find release."

"Exactly," answered Krishna. "You must detach your association with the ego and place it within the Self ..."

"Which already exists beyond the reach of material existence," Arjuna added. "and always has."

"You have it!" said Krishna. "I told you we would get there. Now that you have the first part of the solution, now that you have solved the first piece of the puzzle, we need to concentrate on the second half, which is to enter the consciousness of the higher Self. In order to do so, you need a deeper understanding of Its nature. You need a better idea of what It is like, where you can find It, and so on. And you need to understand the role It plays in My overall being. This is what I would like to go into now."

"Please do!" Arjuna pleaded. "I am ready."

"Keep in mind," said Krishna, "that I am now simply elaborating, simply going into more detail on a subject that I have previously introduced."

"I will keep that in mind," said Arjuna.

"There is a Tree of Life, Arjuna, an everlasting Tree, whose roots are in Heaven and whose branches extend into the realm of physical existence. Off the branches bloom Nature, the gunas, the senses, and the objects of the senses. From this Tree is this world created, nourished, and experienced."

"Okay," said Arjuna. "I see the analogy you are going for."

"The branches are temporary. They come and they go. But the root is eternal." Krishna continued.

"I am with you," said Arjuna. "Spirit is like the root, while the body and the lower mind are like the branches."

"Close," said Krishna. "You are correct, but know this: I am beyond both. I am the Source from which even the root obtains existence. Think of the root as still a part of Karma, the source of Nature, the source of the gunas."

"I did not see that coming," Arjuna admitted. "I thought you were the root."

"I am," said Krishna. "And I am also the branch. But in the end, I am also beyond both. What I am has no concept within the human mind."

"We are back to complexity," Arjuna complained. "This is a difficult concept to grasp."

"It is okay," said Krishna. "You will get there. Going back to the analogy of the virtual reality video game, I would be the world the game takes place within, all of the characters, yet also the creator of the game along with all its components as well."

"Well," said Arjuna. I think I understand a little bit better, but only a little."

"When you permanently enter the Self," said Krishna, "you will understand. Caught up within human consciousness, I am unknowable. It is only from the higher level of consciousness that I can truly be known."

"Okay," said Arjuna. "Then please go on."

"The unripened are completely unaware of the Tree. They only know the world before them and cannot fathom a reality beyond. Even those who begin to become aware of the Tree cannot conceive of how vast and extensive It is—they cannot discern where it begins, where it ends, or just how far Its branches reach. Moving along the Path of Knowledge, they eventually come to conceive of Me as the Tree ... the whole Tree. This is true, yet also untrue, for I am also beyond the tree. The enlightened, the fully ripened know they must escape the Tree's grasp, so they cut it down with detachment, with dissociation from the ego, with dissociation from the gunas and the senses and so escape Its entanglements. They find the root and come to know That which exists beyond the root."

"And one that finds the root, and That which exists beyond," asked Arjuna, "what happens to them?"

"They enter the realm from which one does not return to physical existence," answered Krishna. "Serene, without preference, without desire, free from pleasure and pain, free of joy and suffering, such a one actually enjoys the remainder of his or her days upon this earth, and with the death of the body and the ego they return to the realm of true existence."

"It seems to me," Arjuna noted, "that we have returned to the subject of duality. This world is a duality, made up of pleasure and pain, near and far, high and low, male and female, but beyond the duality is a Unity. From the One came the Two. To reenter the One, one must move beyond the Two."

"Exactly," said Krishna. "But the duality extends a bit further beyond what we have previously discussed. There is an individual soul, a perishable soul, called the ego, and there is also a higher Soul called the Self. Yet beyond even these two, I am. Further, there is a root and a branch, the first existing in Eternity and the other existing in the physical realm. Beyond these two as well, I am. And so are you."

"Boy," said Arjuna. "It just gets deeper and deeper."

"You will get there, Arjuna," assured Krishna, "just stay with Me."

"I plan to," said Arjuna.

"Free from duality in *all* its forms, you find Eternity, You find Me. Find Me, and your task upon this earth is completed."

"Go on," said Arjuna.

"A spark of My eternal Soul, a Spark of the One, an infinitesimal fragment of My being enters this world as the individual Soul. As It does, it becomes entangled in the branches. It becomes entangled in the gunas and the senses. Entangled as It is, caught up in the senses of sight, smell, touch, sound, and taste, the Soul forgets Its eternal nature and becomes fascinated with the physical world. A kind of 'Spiritual amnesia' is the result."

"Like the video game?" Arjuna asked. "The Soul is eternal, it is the entity *playing* the game, not the character within the game. But the individual forgets this and thinks they are the

143

character within the game, which is actually, in this analogy, the finite ego? Is that what you are saying? That we get so tangled up within the branches of the game, so tangled up within the senses, so tangled up within the ongoing dramas of the physical world that we forget our eternal nature? We forget we are not actually within the game, only playing it?"

"Yes," Krishna answered. "That is what I am saying. Yet deep within, beyond the branch, and even beyond the root, is the Self, the Watcher, the Knower. Find the Watcher and you find the individual Soul. Find the individual Soul and the Soul of All comes into view. Free of the bonds of this world, I actually *enjoy* material existence. Find Me, and you will finally be able to do the same. You too will finally be able to enjoy the senses and the sense objects of material existence. Such a one, like Me, is completely free. Presiding over the senses, no longer trapped within them, I and thee will be able to actually *enjoy* contact with the gunas, enjoy contact with the senses, enjoy contact with the sense objects. Together we will be able to create, participate and experience this world as an artist enjoys creating and experiencing his or her own works without being trapped within them."

"I think I understand," said Arjuna.

"You are getting there," Krishna confirmed. "I enjoy this world through you, through all that exists, and through Nature as well. Deep within the hearts of all, I am—you are. You are made in My likeness, Arjuna. Not in form but in Consciousness. You are but a fragment of Me, yet your individual Soul reflects My Whole as well. Find the Self and you come to realize It as part of the Whole. Find the Self and you have found the All."

"Go on," said Arjuna.

"The light of the sun is but a poor imitation of My light." Krishna continued. "The brilliance of My Light is unlike anything humans know."

"I have seen your Light," said Arjuna. "And I can testify to the truth of your words. The light of the sun is nothing compared to your Light."

"Just as the light of the earth is a less intense reflection of My own Light, so too is your Soul a less intense reflection of My own. I am Life and the giver of Life. I am Consciousness Itself. I am the individual Knower, yet I am also the Knower of all Knowers. I am the consciousness of the One in the many and of the many in the One. I am breath. I am digestion. I am love and I am lust. I am the source of memory and knowledge, the process of memory and knowledge, and that which is remembered and known. I am the author of all scriptures, the wisdom they contain, and the goal they all allude to."

"Truly," said Arjuna. "There is no end to what You are."

"What *We* are," Krishna corrected. "In order to find Me, you must let go of the ego, let go of the character, and find and enter the viewpoint of the Player, the viewpoint of the Watcher, the viewpoint of the Knower. Here, you will sit back, unattached, as the world spins around and within your body and your ego. Do this long enough and something *even more* magical happens—you will begin to see the connection between your Self and Me—the connection will come into view. Eventually, your consciousness will expand to the point that you merge with and take on the vantage point of the All. Here, you will continue to simply watch, but not from your own, individual vantage point. You will watch this world go round from My vantage point."

"I will take Your vantage point?" asked Arjuna.

"You will," said Krishna. "Reach My level of consciousness and you will have attained full enlightenment. With individual enlightenment, you are no longer attached to the ego or the body, but you still take the vantage point of the individual Self—you still view this world through your individual senses. With full enlightenment, you move beyond even this level of perception. You take on the viewpoint of the Ultimate Watcher, Arjuna, the viewpoint of Ultimate Knower. You experience this world as I do, from the vantage point of All. Here, all remaining connections with your body and ego are lost. All remaining connections with anything are lost. You look on all of creation as I look on, enjoying all but attached to nothing—not a single thing. Achieve this level of consciousness and the task for which you were forced into physical existence to complete will have been accomplished, and you will be free. Completely, totally, and in every way free."

"Whoever realizes the Self, in whom all of life is One,
fears no more."
-The Upanishads

CHAPTER 16

The Inmates

"I am going to switch gears now, so-to-speak," said Krishna. "I am going to talk about the two main groups of people you come in contact with here during your sojourn on earth."

"Whatever You think I need to hear," said Arjuna. "I trust your judgement."

"Good. Then let us continue," said Krishna. "I have said that you are in prison. I have said that material existence is the 'Bad Place'—the Hell of the scriptures."

"I remember," said Arjuna.

"Another analogy would be to compare material existence with an insane asylum. With either analogy, you come in contact with other people—you come in contact with other inmates—and who you associate with can affect your progress along the path."

"So there are certain people you do not want me to associate with?" asked Arjuna.

"Not exactly," Krishna answered. "Let us just say that there are two types of people: those that are working hard to escape the asylum (or already have), and those who are not. Those that are on the road to release can be an inspiration to your own journey. They can be a reminder of what it is that you are attempting to accomplish. They can push you forward in your attempt to get out of prison. Those who are not interested in escape, on the other hand, can be a hindrance.

They often try to pull you back down to their level. They do not yet have the desire to escape, and they do not wish for you to escape either."

"Am I not to associate with these people?" Arjuna asked again.

"I am not saying that," Krishna answered. "I am not saying that at all. I am only saying that you need to be careful, that you need to be on your guard around such people. You can absolutely be around them. You can absolutely befriend them. But they *will* try to pull you back down to their level, so be mindful. You need to make sure that you do not adopt their bad habits, less your own prison sentence be extended."

"In what ways will they try to bring me down to their level?" Arjuna asked.

"They tend to be pessimistic, Arjuna. They tend to think you are wasting your time trying to follow the Path, and do not mind telling you so. They can be insistent, combative in such matters. They tend to be self-centered and egotistical. They tend to see your efforts at helping others as weak and silly, and may give you a hard time for it. They tend to be fiercely and angrily opinionated and get upset when you do not take their side. They like arguing over religion. They like arguing over politics. In short, they like to argue over anything they can think of, and they can be belligerent in their efforts to push their opinions on you."

"I see what you mean," said Arjuna. "I have already experienced such behaviors."

"Even if they cannot coerce you into their beliefs," Krishna continued, "their efforts can still be disturbing to a mind that is trying to obtain peace. They are still in the stage of tamas. Further, the need for companionship is strong for humans. It is easy to fall prey to peer pressure. Seeing you trying to be good, the ignorant will often endeavor to entice you into their own bad behaviors. Their insistence, and your desire to fit in, can be powerful allies in their efforts to pull you off track."

"I have experienced that as well," Arjuna admitted.

"The bottom line," said Krishna, "is that it is difficult to be around such people and still maintain your focus. Do not get me wrong," said Krishna. "you are to love them and to serve them as best you can. You just need to be careful that you do not let them into your headspace. Such people serve their purpose here on earth, as do all. In fact, they serve as obstacles I have placed in your way to make the journey more difficult. But at your level of consciousness, it is time that you know the part they play and what you can do to avoid being dragged down by them. Even a seeker that has reached a fairly high level of achievement can find it difficult to remain detached from their ego when someone is trying to argue with them, coerce them into bad behavior, or even instigate fights with them."

"I understand," said Arjuna.

"Ultimately, in the end, such a person is the very test you need to solidify the strength of your conviction, the strength of your focus. They serve as a test of your progress, a test of your commitment to the path, and can lift you higher, just as a strong opposing wind lifts a kite into the sky. But until you reach a bit higher of a level, until your enlightenment deepens just a little more, you need to keep in mind that such people can also be a major stumbling block."

"Okay," said Arjuna. "I will remember."

"It is a battle of wills," Krishna went on. "Your will needs to be stronger than theirs to avoid being drawn down But remember at all times, Arjuna, that they are not evil. They are ignorant and scared, trapped in darkness. They will rise in consciousness, as you did, over many incarnations. For now, they are simply operating from a lower level of consciousness. It helps to realize this. They are not enemies, but they are to be guarded against nonetheless. They are not bad, they are only afraid. They do not want you to leave them. They want you to stay at their level."

"Then what do I need to do?" asked Arjuna.

"Love them," Krishna answered. "Befriend them. Just do not *become* them. Do not let their level impede your own progress. You cannot live your life in isolation, and I do not want you to. Part of the test is for you to find Me despite all the obstacles I have placed in your way. At your level of achievement, dark-dwelling people are simply a major impediment, and I want you to be aware of them."

"I am with you," said Arjuna.

"You need to be able to recognize darkness when you see it, Arjuna. And you need to be able to recognize wisdom as well. When you feel yourself slipping, you may need to avoid the dark ones and seek out the wise, at least for a time. Later, once enlightenment has deepened, the ignorant are a good test for your progress. They serve as 'petty tyrants'."

"Petty tyrants?" Arjuna asked.

"Petty tyrants are tests for your progress along the path," Krishna explained. "They are trivial irritations that tell you how far you have travelled. When you can endure the 'petty tyrants' of your life with no ill-effect on your state of mind, you know the end of your journey is near."

"I see. And how can I tell the difference between the two groups of people?" Arjuna asked.

"It is common sense, really," Krishna answered. "For the most part, you already know the answer, you already know the difference between the wise and the ignorant. But to be thorough, let us go into more detail."

"Please do," said Arjuna.

"Okay," said Krishna, "But keep in mind that neither group is absolute. There are different degrees of ignorance, and there are different degrees of wisdom. Telling the two groups apart is not as simple as memorizing the attributes of each group. Instead, each person in either group exists along a gradient of either ignorance or wisdom. The extreme members of either group are the easiest to discern. Where it gets harder is in trying to discern the individuals that do not exist at either end of the spectrum, but somewhere in between."

"I understand," said Arjuna. "It seems that we are back to tamas, rajas and sattva."

"We are. In general," Krishna continued, "the wise live beyond egocentric ideals. They try to help others. They tend to be optimistic. They tend to be truthful, generous, sincere, and open. They tend to be fair and compassionate. They exhibit self-restraint from greed and temptation. They do not argue over frivolous matters. Nor do they stubbornly insist on their own ego-driven viewpoints. Instead, they truly seek knowledge, truly seek the truth in all matters and will listen to the viewpoints of others. They help all life forms and go out of their way to do so, even when it is not in their own best interests. They tend to be patient and avoid criticizing others. They tend to be modest, humble, and gentle. They love all and are kind to all, even those that are not kind or loving to them. The highest ideals they can imagine go beyond the treasures and pleasantries of this world. Their demeanors raise the vibrational level of their consciousness. As this happens, love and knowledge are the result. And you can see this in every aspect of their being."

"And the ignorant?" asked Arjuna.

"They are just the opposite," Krishna answered. "Their vibrational level is slower, which roots them into ignorance and darkness. In general, they tend to be self-centered, sometimes cruel, depending on just how low their level of consciousness is. They live only for their own best benefit. They tend to be pessimistic. They tend to be deceitful, stingy, and insincere. They like drama, and give in to their greed—they do not exhibit self-restraint. They enjoy arguing over frivolous matters. They do not truly seek knowledge in any matter but instead stubbornly insist on their own ego-driven viewpoints. They rarely go out of their way to help others, especially when it is not in their personal best interests. They tend to be impatient and fault-finding in others, but never with themselves. They are typically arrogant, conceited and harsh. They can imagine nothing greater than themselves and truly love themselves alone. They enjoy having opinions and bothering others with them. Even if you agree with them on a point, Arjuna, they may still wish to argue. The highest aim they can imagine is sensual—the acquisition of earthly treasures and earthly pleasantries. Again, they will eventually undertake the journey, they will eventually ripen, but for now they are trapped within the self-made prison of the ego."

"So you are saying," asked Arjuna, "that being able to recognize the ignorant from the wise is another tool I can use to further my progress along the path? That when I find myself falling back into darkness, it is best to seek out the wise and avoid the ignorant, or at least guard myself from them? At least until I am strong enough that I am ready to truly test myself against their ways."

"That is it," Krishna answered. "The ignorant will challenge you every step of your journey. They seek you out and test you. The world is designed this way—I designed it this way. You will always have petty tyrants, you will always be tested. Always. They are attracted to seekers as a moth is attracted to the flame. It is My (and your) way of gauging your progression along the path towards realization of Me."

"So it is Your doing?" asked Arjuna. "You meant for it to be this way?"

"I did," Krishna answered. "Recognizing petty tyrants for what they are and developing a way to cope with them is part of the process of awakening. At lower levels of consciousness, you are unable to think your way through the obstacles and frustrations placed before you. You get angry and frustrated when you face them but never attempt to recognize or analyze the issue at hand, or attempt to think your way through to a real solution. This is a sign that you are still living mostly from the knee-jerk reactionary state of the subconscious mind, or tamas. As awareness blooms, as you begin to move first into the conscious level, or rajas, and then into the Superconscious levels, or sattva, of your mind. You become better and better equipped to recognize the situation for what it is, and to develop a method of overcoming the situation. But remember, once again, that you are to love the petty tyrants every bit as much as you love the wise. I am only saying that you need to recognize them for what they are, and if you find yourself slipping, you may need to take a break and surround yourself with the wise, whose presence can help lift you back onto the path. At the very least, this will give you a break from the constant challenge of the unenlightened."

"I see," said Arjuna. After a few moments of contemplation, he thought of another question. "The religious, are they wise? Is that who I am to seek out?"

"Not necessarily," Krishna answered. "For many, religion is just another trap of the ego. They often use religion to exonerate their own preferences, and prejudices, and beliefs. They tend to think that only their religion is correct, that only their race is correct, that only their nationality is correct, only their denomination is correct. They shun and persecute those that are not of their own race, creed, or color. More blood has been spilled in the name of religion than for any other reason. Do you think this is pleasing to Me?"

"No," Arjuna said. "I do not think that at all."

"Such actions," Krishna explained, "are not of my creation but the creation of humankind. To be sure, there are those that are religious that are also wise. They have found in the words of their scriptures the very love and knowledge I am leading you to. Still, many that claim to be religious are trapped in the very ego that must be shed in order to find Me even though such people believe themselves to be on the path of righteousness. Yet there are also those who are not religious, or do not consider themselves to be, who are wise, who have found love, who have found knowledge. Though they do not claim to be religious, or consider themselves to be, in My eyes they are. Religious leanings are not, in-and-of-itself, a gauge of wisdom."

"Like you said before, even the atheists and agnostics can find you," Arjuna stated. "Just along a different path. A non-spiritually associated path."

"Yes," said Krishna. "If they find love, if they find knowledge, they find Me. They have simply been born with a personality that does not allow them to interpret what they find in a religious manner. I gave them that personality, Arjuna. How can I turn around and punish them for what is out of their control? I am fair. I am just. In whatever way I am found, I accept."

"Got it," said Arjuna. "Love, not dogma; knowledge, not ego, regardless of religious affiliation, persuasion, or orientation—or even a lack thereof."

"Correct," said Krishna. "That is it!"

*"You cannot travel the path until you become the path.
You are not punished for your anger, you are punished
by your anger. Likewise, there is no path to happiness;
happiness itself is the path."*
-Buddha (paraphrased)

CHAPTER 17

The Three Divisions

"Continuing along the lines of the previous conversation," Arjuna began, "I have a question. You said that even those who are not religious may still find You through love or knowledge, correct."

"Correct," Krishna confirmed.

"Which guna prevails in such a person?" Arjuna asked. "Sattva, rajas, or tamas: goodness, passion, or darkness?"

"In our previous discussion," Krishna began, "I used two divisions to define the people you come into contact with while here on earth: those who were seeking the path to liberation, and those who, as of yet, were not. Using the three divisions of the gunas is a more thorough example, so it is good that you brought it up. To answer your question, there is not just one guna that prevails in non-religious people."

"There is not?" asked Arjuna.

"No," said Krishna. "Just like anyone else, those of non-religious inclinations begin their journey in tamas, move into rajas, and eventually complete their journey in sattva. I hinted at this in our last conversation. This progression occurs over the course of many incarnations, though the progression is evident to a lesser extent within each individual incarnation as well."

"Please explain," said Arjuna. "I think that last statement confused me."

"Let us begin with the *overall* progression of consciousness," said Krishna. "As I have said, over the course of many lifetimes, the consciousness of each individual expands from the lower levels of tamas into the intermediate levels of rajas and finally into the upper levels of sattva."

"I think I understand that part," said Arjuna. "Over the course of many lifetimes, we mature or ripen into higher levels of awareness and compassion."

"Correct," Krishna continued. "However, the same progression also occurs within each individual lifetime, just on a much smaller scale. Each person, no matter what level they have reached overall, is born into each individual lifetime as an infant, for the most part unaware. This is the stage of tamas, the lowest level of consciousness. As he or she ages, their awareness begins to grow and they enter the stage of rajas. Towards the end of each person's life, their awareness and comprehension and mental abilities tend to have progressed to the point that they enter sattva. However, this progression through individual lifetimes is not the same as the overall progression, though it definitely adds to it. The smaller cycles of growth within each lifetime mirror and add to the larger cycles of growth that occur over successive lifetimes."

"I think I am beginning to get it," said Arjuna. "On the smaller scale, as one experiences life, consciousness or awareness increases, which moves us from the tamas of childhood into the rajas of adulthood and eventually the sattva of old age. On a larger scale, the same evolution occurs over the course of many lifetimes. Is this correct?"

"It is," said Krishna. "You progress through smaller cycles of the gunas *during each lifetime* and through larger cycles *with each successive incarnation.* Think of it as interlinked smaller cycles within larger cycles of expanding awareness. Each lifetime lived adds to the overall enhancement of consciousness."

"So with each life lived," Arjuna asked, "we start at a higher level of consciousness than the level we started at in the previous incarnation?"

"That is correct," said Krishna. "As I have said before, no progression is ever lost."

"Okay," Arjuna said, "But to clarify, even if we have a person who has attained the level of sattva overall, they are still born into the next individual existence, the next small cycle, at a level of tamas?"

"Yes, *but ...*" said Krishna. "their level of tamas will not be as deep or dark in this lifetime as someone whose overall level is tamas. Do you not know children who seem advanced for their age?"

"I do," said Arjuna.

"This is why," Krishna explained. "They are in the smaller cycle of tamas in their current life, but they are in sattva overall, which makes them wise for their age. And when they reach the level of rajas, it is the same thing—the traits of rajas will not be as obvious as they are in someone who is at an overall level of rajas. Further, when a person of overall sattva reaches the level of sattva in this individual lifetime ... well, that's when the magic happens. That is when a person is ready to hear from Me. This is the level that you have obtained."

"So, I have matured in consciousness to the level of sattva overall," Arjuna noted, "And I have also matured in this lifetime to the level of sattva. The two combined is why I am ready for Your instruction."

"That, Arjuna, is exactly it! Cycles within cycles. All is interconnected. Each person has an overall level of attainment, but each person also passes through the three levels of attainment during this existence as well. A person of tamas goes through the earthly cycles of tamas, rajas and sattva in this incarnation. A person of rajas does the same, as does the person of sattva. It is the combined overall guna each person has attained, mixed with the earthly cycle they are going through that, combined in unique ways, create each person's individual level of consciousness."

"You know what?" Arjuna asked. "I think I actually get it. Each person is at a specific level overall, but also, to a lesser extent, cycle through the three gunas during each earthly existence as well. The combination is what decides the predominant guna of each individual."

"You have understood well," said Krishna. "And I am well pleased. But I need to instruct you a little further. There is a little more you need to know for full comprehension."

"Then please continue," said Arjuna.

Krishna continued. "The three gunas define how each individual views and experiences reality. The guna of each person determines his or her beliefs and behaviors. As a person *is*, so they *perceive*, so they *believe*, and so they *act*. Whatever viewpoint that person has, that viewpoint defines their world. Each person experiences reality not as *it* is, but as *they* are.

The gunas are, therefore, another way of measuring each person's progress along the path to higher consciousness."

"So each person's guna defines how they view and act in the world?" asked Arjuna.

"Yes," said Krishna. "And by understanding how the gunas affect a person's beliefs and behaviors, we are able to gauge each person's level of consciousness. For example, let us talk about temperament. The person of sattva is pure and open and compassionate. They work for the betterment of all, and in doing so, begin to rise above their egos. The person of rajas is passionate. They are still stuck in an intense association with the ego (though less so than a person of tamas) and are filled with egotistical needs and desires. They work, but mostly for their own gratification. The person of tamas is almost completely stuck in darkness, completely stuck in ego. They do not wish to work. They feel existence owes them a living and refuse to do much of anything on their part to achieve any level of success. There is barely a thing that exists outside of ego for a person of tamas."

"Got it," Arjuna said. "And the level of guna each person expresses depends not just on the guna they are experiencing in this lifetime, but is also influenced by the overall attainment they have achieved. A person of tamas, for example, may still experience sattva towards the end of this incarnation, but they will not exhibit the same level of goodness or pureness as that expressed by a person of overall sattva. And a person of overall sattva may still experience the passion of rajas during this lifetime, but will not exhibit the same level of passion and egotism as the person who is at a lower level of consciousness overall—say of tamas or rajas."

"You have it," said Krishna. "Continuing, the person of sattva cannot imagine harming another, The person of rajas might, if it is in their best interest, but this usually does not include violence or murder. Instead, they may, for example, find money and not return it. Or cheat someone in a business transaction. Or commit adultery. The person of tamas, on the other hand, *can* be violent. They may even be capable of murder. They are capable of harming or even killing animals or possibly people if they so see fit, not knowing that their aggression, in the end, is aimed at Me."

"Aimed at You?" Arjuna asked.

"I exist within all, Arjuna," Krishna answered. "I am the Essence within all beings."

"Okay," said Arjuna. "I think I understand.

"Stuck within tamas," Krishna elaborated, "a person is thoroughly trapped within the sense of 'I' and 'mine', and is driven by warped, wordly perceptions and desires. Once that person reaches rajas, the ego begins to fade, but only a little. For the person of rajas, other people at least exist and have needs, but their own individual needs usually take precedence. Only the person of sattva has begun to rise fully above the ego and begun to see the truth."

"Got it," said Arjuna.

"To solidify your understanding of the gunas," Krishna went on, "and the interrelatedness of all things, let us discuss the gunas as they pertain to food."

"To food?" asked Arjuna, confused.

"Yes," Krishna answered. "This will all tie in. Do not worry."

"Okay," said Arjuna.

"Food whose main characteristic is sattvic is fresh, pure and nutritious. When eaten, sattvic food promotes health, vitality, strength, a clean body, a clear mind, and longevity. Sattvic people tend to be drawn to sattvic foods."

"Sattvic people are drawn to eating sattvic foods?" Arjuna questioned.

"Yes," said Krishna. "This is but one example of the interrelationship of the gunas in all aspects of material existence. Like sattvic food, a sattvic person is pure and good, and they tend to be drawn toward foods that are, likewise, pure and good. Like attracts like, remember?"

"I do," said Arjuna.

"Have you not noticed that the younger or less educated a person is, which is the stage of tamas, the more they prefer junk food?"

"I have," Arjuna admitted. "now that you mention it. "And as one ages, or becomes educated, they tend to gravitate towards vegetables and clean eating. They tend to become interested in diet, exercise, and all things healthy."

"Exactly!" said Krishna. "They are moving from tamas towards rajas and eventually sattva. Moving on, let us discuss rajas-type foods. Food predominantly containing the nature of rajas tends to be acidic and sharp, or salty and dry. These foods build strength, but the strength they offer is not pure—it is inconsistent and overall unhealthy. Rajas-type foods can give you power, but they also clog the body and mind. They lead to heaviness, illness and pain. Rajas-type people tend to prefer, or tend to be drawn to, rajas-type foods and diets."

"I am catching on," said Aruna. "Please go over tamas-type food."

"Tamas-type foods are processed and stale," Krishna explained. "They tend to be devoid of nutrients but filled with calories. Such foods are impure. They contain excessive amounts of salt, additives, and preservatives. They tend to be overloaded with sugar, which is designed to make the food taste better, and chemicals, which are designed to make the food last longer. Processed foods and junk foods are good examples, Arjuna. These are foods that are no longer in their natural state, foods that are no longer fresh, foods that have been altered in some way."

"So, fresh food is better than preserved foods?" asked Arjuna.

"Yes," said Krishna. "Preserved, processed foods are filled with toxins and calories but are nearly devoid of any actual nourishment. These are the types of food a person of tamas—usually the young, the uneducated, the unripe—tend to prefer. Just as their minds have not developed the taste for the pure and everlasting treasures of spiritual pursuits, so too have their palates not developed the desire for pure foods. All is related, Arjuna. All the things of this world work together in unison."

"As I am beginning to realize!" said Arjuna.

"The same goes for sound," said Krishna. "Children and those of tamas overall are noisy and enjoy loud music. This preference gradually diminishes over each lifetime to the point that, in old age, one tends to prefer soothing music over loud and turbulent, or even silence over all else."

"I have definitely noticed this," said Arjuna.

"The same goes for actions," Krishna added. "People that have reached the guna of sattva perform actions that are good;

and not just for themselves but for the good of all. They do their duty, want to do their duty, and do not expect a reward in return. The person of rajas works, but mostly for egotistical reward. They do not tend to help those who are truly in need, although they may. Not as much as a person of sattva, but they are beginning to advance a little beyond purely egotistical gain. Usually though, they tend to help those from whom they think they can expect a reward."

"What kind of reward?" asked Arjuna.

"Praise, glory, honor, sex, good-standing in society," Krishna answered, "or material reward."

"Yeah. I can see that," said Arjuna.

"The person of tamas," Krishna continued, "tends toward laziness. When they do act, they do so completely and totally out of self interest. They will lie, cheat, and steal to get whatever it is they feel they are entitled to. Thus, Arjuna, can you tell the level of guna a person has attained by their actions."

"And by the foods and level of noise they prefer," Arjuna added.

"Exactly," said Krishna. "The gunas influence *all* phenomena of this realm. But keep in mind that I am not giving you this tool so it can be used to judge another, at least not in the context of judging another as right or wrong, good or bad. I am giving you this tool for understanding consciousness levels so that you can gauge your own progress, and so that you can be aware of those who exist at lower levels of consciousness. There is no judgment here, only the understanding that you may need to guard your mind against those of lower levels, lest they bring you down in your progress."

"I understand," said Arjuna. "I am to love them, not judge them, but I also need to be aware of the influence they can have over me. They will progress, just as I did, but for now, their minds still operate from lower levels of awareness."

"Exactly," said Krishna.

"Are there other examples of the guna's influence that would help me?"

"There are endless examples, Arjuna," Krishna said. "I will go over a couple of others, but remember, the gunas influence *all* behavior in this realm."

"I will keep that in mind," said Arjuna.

"Worship, for example," Krishna continued, "performed by a person of sattva is genuine, but of rajas and tamas is done so out of hopes for an individual, egotistical gain. Likewise, gifts given by the person of sattva are also genuine, but those given by the person of rajas or tamas are given with the intent of gaining some kind of return."

"So, all things of this world follow this pattern," Arjuna stated. "*All* things."

"Yes," said Krishna. "They do."

"I *am* beginning to understand," said Arjuna. "But this is definitely a complex subject. It is hard to gain a firm grasp on it. There are attributes of each guna that are fairly easy to discern, but it is still not straightforward, for there are cycles within cycles to consider."

"Exactly," said Krishna. "This is why what I am about to tell you is so important, so listen well."

"I will," said Arjuna.

"In the end, the key to all I have told you in all of our discussions, including the gunas of this conversation, can be summed up very simply with the phrase 'OM TAT SAT'. If you find the details of My teachings too complex or too confusing, just remember this phrase and its meaning, and you may still obtain understanding."

"OM TAT SAT?" Arjuna repeated. "Please explain the phrase for me."

"I have, this entire time," Krishna said, "been summarizing the entirety of eons of My teachings for you. I have distilled the general principles of all My teachings into seventeen discussions so far. Yet even these summaries can be summed up succinctly by the single phrase: OM TAT SAT. A true understanding of its meaning is the ultimate key to unlocking the door to liberation. It stands for the absolute truth that *I Am All That is.* These three words also encapsulate the three individual manifestations of My being—the best it can be encapsulated for the human mind—and is the key, the code, for unlocking the vault of knowledge that guards against the comprehension of the Ultimate, and therefore the attainment of liberation."

"Then please go on," said Arjuna. "Please explain its meaning."

"OM," said Krishna, "is the vibration or sound of God. It is the primordial vibration of creation, the Word of God that created and runs this world of form."

"I am with you. And TAT," asked Arjuna.

"TAT translates as 'that'," Krishna answered, "and it symbolizes Universal Consciousness. I am Consciousness Itself. All that is has consciousness because I exist within all that is. I am That which knows It is. And so are you. It is God within you that allows you to know that you are, that allows you to know that you exist, that allows you to have experiences and allows you to know that you have those experiences."

"And SAT," asked Arjuna.

"SAT means 'truth'," Krishna responded, "and represents the Supreme Soul, the Ultimate—it represents My Being."

"It sounds like we have returned to the idea of the Trinity," said Arjuna. "Three different aspects of God that are, in the end, actually One."

"You are correct," said Krishna. "The Trinity has been known and discussed in various forms throughout all the major religions. It represents the three different manifestations of Spirit in terms of vibration, consciousness, and being. If you prefer, you can refer to these aspects as the Father, the Son and the Holy Spirit. But yes, you are correct. The Trinity represents the three separate entities of reality that are, in reality, One and the same. Realize that I am all that is, realize that the three powers are actually One, realize that all worlds, in the end, are actually One, that they all come from and are formed from Me, and your mind may just be able to achieve an inkling of the Ultimate Truth."

"I think I understand!" said Arjuna. "You exist as Being, Consciousness, *and* Vibration. You are the Ultimate Being. Your Being has and is made up of Consciousness Itself, and You give consciousness to all that exists. You create and run the material world of form through varying rates of Vibration, also referred to as the 'Word of God', which emanates from Your Being and Your Consciousness. All beings are, in the end, Your being. All consciousness, in the end, is Your consciousness. And all forms, ultimately, is Your form, created from the differing levels of vibration emanating from Your being. Yet these separations do not actually exist, for in reality, they are all You. They are all One and the same. Is this correct?"

"Yes, Arjuna," said Krishna. "This is what I have been trying to impart to you this entire time. Ultimately, what this means, in concrete usable terms, is that *all* that exists is Me. If you can view the entirety of life, all that you have come to know of it—mental or physical, material or energetic, on earth or in the farthest reaches of space—as a single entity, you are almost there. Work for Me, Arjuna. Work for the betterment of All, as a duty unto Me. Live not for yourself but for the good of All, and, because, once again, like attracts like, your individual level of vibration, your individual level of consciousness, and your individual level of being will approach and merge back into that of My own. In working for others, you are surrendering all of your actions unto Me. When everything you think or do or see becomes centered not around yourself but around the betterment of All, your very life becomes an ode to Glory. Your very existence becomes a worship unto Me. From that point on, all you perceive will be Me."

"Give Light, and the darkness will disappear of itself."
-Erasmus

CHAPTER 18

Surrender

"As I have previously explained," Krishna began, "I have, over the course of our discussions, attempted to summarize and encapsulate the intricacies of eons of My teachings into a more condensed, palatable and digestible form. Still, I know that, even in its most simplified and summarized form the Truth is vast, complex, and extremely difficult to grasp."

"To say the least," said Arjuna.

"What I would like to do now, in our final conversation," Krishna continued, "is go back over a few of the main points, as well as go into further detail on those aspects of My instructions that seekers seem to have had the most problems with in the past. I will then end our discussions by going back over the failsafe I mentioned in past discussions— the backdoor I put in place in order to allow relief from the confines of this world for those who find all other means of escape insurmountable."

"Please do!" said Arjuna. "Please go on!"

"The first area I would like to touch upon deals with walking the Path while still living within and taking part of this world. Some believe that to be spiritual, they must renounce *all* worldly activities. Monks, for example, as I have already mentioned, often feel this way. They avoid worldly activities and spend most of their time in meditation or prayer. They do not take spouses, do not produce children, and often do not work. They do so because they feel all worldly phenomena to be a distraction to their progress. They feel that having a spouse may lead to unnecessary temptations involving lust. They feel that having children may lead to unhealthy attachments. They feel that having a job may tempt them with greed and possibly even deceit."

"But renunciation of life itself is not the Way." stated Arjuna.

"No, it is not," said Krishna. "I place the very obstacles before you that you need to face in order for you to mature into the next level of attainment. You are supposed to be tempted by lust. You are supposed to be tempted by attachment. You are supposed to be tempted by greed. If you refuse to participate in life, how will you ever face and eventually grow beyond such obstacles? *The obstacle is the path.* Each person *must* be tempted by these things before they will be able to realize, as you eventually did, that they have no lasting value. Before you can develop a desire for the divine, you must first grow weary of the temptations of this world. In order to do that, you must first experience them."

"But you said I may need to be aware of those around me that could impede my progress," said Arjuna. "That I may need to avoid them, at least for a time"

"Be aware, yes," said Krishna, "Avoid such people for a time, sure. But you cannot avoid life altogether. You may need a rest here and there, but you cannot, by any means, avoid living in general. You are here to grow and expand and mature in consciousness, but to do so requires experience. How are you to learn and advance and ripen without actually experiencing anything? Life is nothing but long and repeating cycles of trial and error through which each person eventually obtains mastery and wisdom over all that has been holding them back from Me."

"I see," said Arjuna. "And I understand."

"Continuing," said Krishna, "There is another reason you must participate in life. You are here to mature, which is for your sake. But you are also here to contribute a verse to the Song of Life," Krishna continued. "You are here to be of use to Me and to all that lives. You are to use your individual talents to contribute to My creation. This is why I gave each of you such talents in the first place. I use each individual's talents in the way that best fits My overall purpose, my overall design, not your own. I use you, all of you, to evolve My creation, to carry out My plan for the betterment of all. To refuse to contribute is a form of selfishness. I work and so must you, it is as simple as that."

"I understand that as well," said Arjuna.

"What I am getting at," Krishna went on, "is that it is not life that needs to be renounced, only your attachment to living it selfishly. It is your attachment to your body, your attachment to your ego, your attachment to wealth and acclaim and all other selfish pursuits that I ask you to give up, not life itself. You are here to learn, to evolve beyond what you see before you, and to find That which exists within. The only way to do this is to face the trials and tribulations and temptations I place before you. Do so and you will eventually tire of them, you will eventually overcome them, you will eventually outgrow them. No one will ever tire of them or overcome or outgrow them by merely avoiding them altogether. You are to live, Arjuna. To live and learn and love despite all the setbacks and disappointments of this world. Do you understand?"

"I do," said Arjuna. "You gave us our individual attributes and talents, and we are to use them in service to the world, in service to You, not solely for our own benefit. By living, by facing the trials and tribulations of life, we not only contribute to Your creation, as we are required to do, but in the process we also encounter the very obstacles that will eventually challenge us to move beyond them and ultimately elevate us into higher and higher levels of consciousness and self-mastery."

"Exactly," said Krishna. "Even the most praiseworthy action must eventually be done with no concern whatsoever for individual results. It must be done simply because it must be done. Understand?"

"I do," said Arjuna.

"Good," said Krishna. "Then let us move on. In an earlier discussion we used the term renunciation. I said you were to renounce your ego and the results of your works, not renounce life itself. Still, some seekers have had trouble with this term. A better word for what you need to do would be surrender. Surrender is the relinquishing of motive and reward and ego. It is surrender that I require of you, not the renunciation of life Itself. It is surrender that elevates you on the Path and it is the renunciation of life that keeps you where you are. The end of your journey comes when you figure out how to *be* in this world and *contribute* to this world without being *of* this world. Understand? You are the consciousness within you, Arjuna, not the body or ego that you have become so attached to. The divinity you seek is your own mind. Realize this and the journey is over. Realize this and you have returned home—you have returned to Me, for I am your mind, I am your home."

"We are clear," said Arjuna, wiping a tear from his eye. "I understand."

"Next, we need to go into your status as a warrior on the battlefield of life," said Krishna.

"Okay," said Arjuna. "I am ready."

"Many find life to be weary and without reward," said Krishna, "which is another reason so many refuse to participate. Some do this because they exist within the level of tamas, which makes them lazy, and fearful, and selfish. They feel entitled and see no point in participation. They see the trials and tribulations before them and go weak. The person of rajas is fully engaged in life, but for reasons that are tied to the ego. They are passionate about striving in order to obtain all those things of this world they find precious. Others, like you when we first spoke, have fought the battle; they have moved through the darkness of tamas and the passion of rajas and finally moved into sattva. In doing so, they have found this world to be empty or devoid of any real treasure. Such a person has seen this world for what it is, which is good, but they have yet to see That which is beyond, and so become weary and despondent as well. This is the 'Dark Night of the Soul'. They, like the person of tamas, may try to escape their duties as a warrior. They, like the person of tamas, may try to avoid life altogether. In either scenario, the battle is difficult but it goes on, whether you willingly participate or not. There is no being on the face of this earth who can fully avoid or renounce living. While of this earth, action is imperative; it is unavoidable. The resolution to renounce living is in vain for

Nature *will* compel you to fight, *I* will compel you to fight, to persist, whether you wish to do so or not. Bound by body, bound by ego, bound by Karma, there is no choice but to go on, there is no choice but to fight, so fight you *must*. There is no way to avoid the battle—there is no escape. Sooner or later you must face the war you were born to fight. When you find yourself in Hell, Arjuna, keep moving forward. The worst thing you can do when you find yourself in Hell is to stand still, to remain where you are."

"I understand," said Arjuna. "I cannot avoid living, and I am not supposed to. But I am to live without attachment to the ego, without attachment to worldly desires. I am to surrender my life to the betterment of all, not renounce my life altogether."

"Exactly," said Krishna. "In doing so, you find and walk the path that leads to Moksha—the path that leads to liberation, the path that leads to emancipation. No mastery is tamas. Mastery of others is rajas. Mastery of the self is sattva—it is the mastery of Life itself. And you, My good and dear friend, have finally arrived at sattva. Deep within there is a voice that does not use words—listen for it, then do as you best see fit. Have you heard Me, Arjuna?"

"I have," said Arjuna.

"Live in the manner I have described and I will deliver you from the suffering of this world. Even while still upon this earth you will have reached freedom, and I promise you that not a single thing will ever be able to touch you, ever again. And at death, your consciousness, your being, will join that of My own. No longer will you be bound to this earth. No longer will you be bound by your body or your ego. No,

Arjuna, live as I have outlined and the chains of your shackles will shatter like glass from the blow of a hammer!"

Weeping, Arjuna thanked Krishna repeatedly for His instruction.

"I have one final lesson for you, Arjuna. And it is the deepest, most important secret I have."

"Is this the failsafe You mentioned before?" Arjuna asked.

"It is," said Krishna. "We have already discussed the matter, more than once, but I would like to go over it again. It is that important."

"Yes, please!" Arjuna entreated.

"If all else fails," Krishna continued. "If you find My teachings too complex or too convoluted to master, there is still one last card to play. If you find attachment to your body, attachment to your ego, or attachment to the things of this world too hard to overcome, I have set in place a failsafe that will still deliver you unto Me. If even the concept of OM TAT SAT is too hard to grasp, find this backdoor and I will come to you Myself. I will personally deliver you from the ills of this world."

"Please!" Arjuna begged. "Please tell me what it is!"

"Love, Arjuna," said Krishna. "The failsafe is love. Find Love and you find Me. Experience Love and you are actually experiencing Me."

"I do love you!" said Arjuna.

"Oh, and how I love you as well!" said Krishna. "Which is why love is the failsafe. My love for you all is so great that I cannot resist one that loves Me in return. I simply cannot. Love Me and the battle is over. Love Me and I will personally rescue you from your prison."

"But all experience love already, do they not," asked Arjuna.

"Yes," Krishna answered, "but only to a limited extent. They may love themselves. They may love their wife or their child or their friends. They may love their dog or their cat. In doing so, they *do* experience Love, they *do* experience Me, but only in limited form. They love only pieces of Me. The limit of one's love for Me is determined by the limit of one's love for others. Grow instead to love *all* that exists, not only those you love naturally, and not only those who are easy to love, and I will come into focus. It is easy to love those you already do. The real test is in loving those that you now see as enemies. Love your neighbor as yourself and the breakthrough comes—I come. That is the real test, that is where I am hidden—just behind your love for *all*. The last morsel of love most people are held back by is the love for their enemies. Love even them and your love will finally have expanded to *all* of Me. Love Me in totality and you will have found Me in *full* form. Such a one I simply cannot resist, Arjuna. I simply cannot! For such a person, the battle is over! The only way you can conquer Me is through love, Arjuna, and there I am gladly conquered."

Arjuna fell to his knees in joy, weeping uncontrollably.

"If all else fails, find love and you find Me. Do so and I give you My word of promise that we will walk this world together, hand-in-hand, out of this realm and into the next."

"And all the trials and tribulations of life?" Arjuna questioned.

"With your eye on the storm," Krishna answered, "you will experience only the storm. With your eye on Me, and only on Me, you will no longer even know the storm exists."

"It sounds like," Arjuna added, "that we are still speaking of surrender."

"We are," Krishna confirmed. "Surrender yourself to the will of Love and you are free. Do so and I will claim you as My own, no questions asked. All sins will be forgiven and you will never suffer again. Take refuge in Me and the battle is won. Leave all else behind, and with an eye only on Me, I will walk you into Heaven. From that moment on you will be free of this world of shadows and puppets, marching ever onward in its illusion of time."

"I understand," said Arjuna, still weeping openly. "I am with you. I am yours. Your will and only Your will be done! I see that now!"

"I will leave you with one last request," said Krishna. "For you are now ready."

"Ready?" asked Arjuna.

"Ready," Krishna answered. "Ready to complete your journey, and ready to become My vessel for leading others. In the beginning I told you to lead only by example. You were not ready to lead in any other way back then, but now you are. My ultimate teachings must not be spoken to those who are not yet ready, but you now know how to recognize those who are ready, and you have now moved beyond any egotistical intent in spreading My message. So go now, Arjuna, live as you feel is correct, and help all of humankind to reach Me. Lighten their suffering. Help them in their journey. For those who are not yet ready for the ultimate knowledge, guide them gently in the correct direction. For those who *are* ready, help them to find Me. Give them the Ultimate. Bring all that exist the same comfort that I have brought you. This is the greatest gift you can give Me, and I ask it of you in earnest. Lead all to Me and I will do the rest, just as I have done for you."

Arjuna nodded that he understood, unable to speak.

"Have you heard Me, Arjuna? Has the darkness truly lifted? Has the Light taken hold?"

"By your grace," Arjuna was finally able to manage, "do I now remember Your Light, do I now remember Your love. The darkness has vanished into illusion and I am overwhelmed with love and awe. All doubts have fallen away! My amnesia has lifted! I remember and my soul is filled with joy and splendor and hope! I will never be the same again, and I truly hope never to be again."

"Go now, my dear, precious Arjuna," said Krishna, "and spread My Word of Promise to all. These are My final words."

"The Lord of Love is the One Self of all. Realize the Self hidden in the heart, and cut asunder the knot of ignorance."
-Mundaka Upanishad

CONSIDER READING NEXT

- The Upanishads 101 (Book One of the Hindu Enlightenment Series)
  Author page: amazon.com/author/matthewbarnes

Or consider starting the Egyptian Enlightenment Series:
- The Emerald Tablet 101
- The Hermetica 101
- The Kybalion 101

Matthew's "Zennish Series" books can be read in any order, but Matthew meant for them to be read in the following order:
- Tao Te Ching 101
- Albert Einstein, Zen Master
- Tao Te Ching 201
- Jesus Christ, Zen Master
- Dr. Seuss, Zen Master
- Willy Wonka, Zen Master
- Mark Twain, Zen Master

Or consider one of MS Barnes' novels:
- Folie¿
- Meet Frank King

*Be warned that Matthew's novels are not the same as his spiritual works, though they do dive heavily into the power of the mind.

REFERENCES

The following are the sources I used in preparing my rendition. These are my favorite overall translations:

- *https://www.scoopify.org/bhagavad-gita-quotes/* is a website that lists the most famous quotes from the Bhagavad Gita. These quotes alone are inspirational and instructional and I highly recommend them.
- *The Bhagavad Gita* by Penguin Classics. This is a great academic interpretation of *The Bhagavad Gita* and one of the main works I referenced for this work. It is definitely worth a read for gaining a deeper understanding of the subject.
- *Bhagavad Gita: A New Translation* by Stephen Mitchell. This is the most beautiful translation of the *Gita* that I have come across. I referenced it often for this work. I honestly did not plan on interpreting the *Gita* because I did not feel I could do a better job than Stephen Mitchell. However, I came to believe that, although I could not produce a more *beautiful* rendition, I felt I may be able to produce a *simpler* one—one that neophytes may find more accessible. Mitchell's translation is a beautiful yet still academic translation, whereas my version is less poetic, less academic, but, I believe, simpler. I *highly* recommend Stephen Mitchell's work.
- *http://www.bhagavad-gita.org*: This is an online explanation of the *Gita* which I also referenced

extensively. The site offers academic interpretations, but each chapter, and the *Gita* overall, is also summarized for enhanced understanding. It is definitely worth looking into.

- There are also quite a few YouTube videos on the *Gita* that are worth seeking out. Many of these videos do a very good job of explaining and simplifying the work. Simply print "Bhagavad Gita simplified" into the the search bar and go.

LETTER FROM THE AUTHOR

Dear Reader,

Thank you for reading my book! You've made my day!
I would very much like to know what you thought of my book and why. If you have time, please leave me a review on Amazon letting me know your thoughts. It doesn't need to be complex. A word or sentence will do. Remember that the number of reviews a book gets and the number of stars a book gets can make or break a book on Amazon, so please be kind.

If you have any questions or comments feel free to email me at Dr.MatthewBarnes12@gmail.com. I promise I will try to respond.

Thank you for spending time with me!

Matthew Barnes

AUTHOR BIO

Matthew Barnes is an avid learner who spent his early years in North Carolina. During college, he experienced a stint with depression which led him to the works of the Eastern philosophers. He started writing simplified versions of the works he was inspired by in response to a friend that was struggling with religion. He hopes his attempts at simplifying the philosophies of ancient spiritual traditions will make them more accessible to Western minds, and in turn, will help bring peace to those, like his friend, who have found themselves lost in a world that, at times, seems so devoid of meaning and hope.

To check the progress on his other works, go to: amazon.com/author/matthewbarnes, or sign up for updates at: https://forms.aweber.com/form/50/1802384050.htm

Made in the USA
Monee, IL
13 April 2025

15709291R00111